THAT TEA BOOK

Patricia Rose Cress

A CIP catalogue record for this book is available from the British Library

Published by
AA Publishing, which is a trading name of Automobile Association Developments Limited whose registered office is Norfolk House, Priestley Road, Basingstoke, Hampshire RG24 9NY, Registered number 1878835.

Produced by AA Publishing

Researched and written by:
Patricia Rose Cress

Cover artwork by:
The Company of Designers, Basingstoke

Printed and bound in Great Britain by:
BPC Paperbacks, Aylesbury

The contents of this book are believed correct at the time of printing. Nevertheless, the Publishers cannot be held responsible for any errors or omissions or for changes in the details given in this guide or for the consequences of any reliance on the information provided in the same. Every effort has been made to ensure accuracy in this guide. However, things do change and we would welcome any information to help keep the book up to date.

Descriptions of places in this guide are based on information supplied in good faith by the establishments in advance of publication and correct to the best of their knowledge at that time. Details, particularly those relating to prices, opening hours and events, are always liable to change.

Contents

Acknowledgements   4

British to a Tea   5

England   7

Scotland   158

Wales   166

Index   175

Acknowledgements

With thanks for their kind contributions

Princess Alexandra
Honor Blackman
Dame Barbara Cartland DBE DStJ
Lorraine Chase
Stephanie Cole
Phil Collins
Tom Courtenay
Lord St John of Fawsley
David Gower
Nigel Hawthorne
Maureen Lipman
Ron Moody
Stirling Moss
Su Pollard
Anton Rodgers
Donald Sinden
Una Stubbs
Emma Tennant
Frankie Vaughan
Terry Wogan
Michael York

This book is dedicated to
everyone everywhere
who loves a good cup of tea

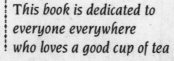

British to a Tea

*Tea rooms are different. Tea rooms are
magic. They cast a spell over me. Nothing
gives me greater pleasure than pushing open
the door of one of my favourites — to the
front, the tea room looks out on to the quietness of a small town square. The back leads
the eye to a garden overflowing with roses. It
is light, airy and delightful, but best of all is
the atmosphere of congeniality, and the
welcoming smile.*

*My favourite words have to be 'shall I put
the kettle on' and if tea comes with scones,
crumpets and chocolate cake, on doilies if
possible, two of my three wishes will have
been granted. My third? An Elvis look-alike
whispering 'one lump or two, sugar'.*

Patricia Rose

Patricia Rose Cress

From: Dame Barbara Cartland, D.B.E., D.St.J.

Tea is and always has been a social drink, at which women particularly enjoy each others company and exchange their special ideas in the way of bringing up their children.

It is romantic in that so many love affairs are started with people have met each other at a Tea Party when a man has found a woman particularly feminine, attractive and exactly the sort of person he wants as his wife.

Personally I find, as I have all my life that the best and most amusing conversations between women take place when they have tea with me and we drink the special Earl Grey tea which I have always found much the nicest and the tastiest.

Barbara Cartland

Mrs Pickwick

High Street, Midsomer Norton
Telephone: (01761) 414589

When you are searching for somewhere that is simple, open and direct, in its food, its style and its place, Mrs Pickwick's fits the bill perfectly. It exudes an air of charming informality-almost like popping into a friend's for a cuppa and a natter. In good weather trundle through to the little pavement terrace.

What to see:

Apart from Bath itself, which needs at least a week to fully explore, the small county of Avon is full of visual interest. The villages and small towns have a lot of appeal because of the county's rich variety of building stone and the countryside which offers differing kinds of landscape, often within just a few miles.

THE TEA:
Potter downstairs for the tea menu Home-made scones with clotted cream go very quickly, accompanied by freshly brewed tea Price: from £2 50

OPEN:
Monday to Saturday from 9 00am to 5.30pm Closed Sunday and Bank Holidays

GETTING THERE:
Midsomer Norton is on the A362 road Parking in the town

Choose thy company before thy drink.

The Pump Room

Stall Street, Bath
Telephone: (01225) 444488

Since the middle of the 18th century the Pump Room has been a favourite Bath meeting place, and remains so to this day. Elegant portraits of early dignitaries adorn the walls, great chandeliers hang from the high ceiling, and during the summer a trio sometimes plays on the galleried podium. It is a perfect setting for afternoon tea.

What to see:

Do see the Pump Room, Roman Baths, and Roman Baths Museum. Also the Assembly Room, Theatre Royal and the Museum of Costume. Claverton Manor, two-and-a-half miles south-east of Bath is now the American Museum in Britain.

THE TEA:
Bath buns, scones with clotted cream, and toast with gentleman's relish are just some of the traditional teatime fare A selection of tea blends is available Price from £4.50.

OPEN:
Monday to Sunday 10 00am to 5.30pm Early closing 4.30pm November to March.

GETTING THERE:
Bath is on the A4 A36 A46 roads Nearest motorway M4. Town car parks

He is at ease who has enough.

Sally Lunn's House

4 North Parade Passage, Bath
Telephone: (01225) 461634

The name Sally Lunn is said to originate from the late 18th century, when Sally Lunn became famous for her home-made tea biscuits and buns which she sold in the streets of Bath. The house is reputedly the oldest in Bath, excavations have revealed Roman occupation.

What to see:

For a general view over the city, walk or drive to Beechen Cliff or climb to Sham Castle. The Bath Festival is held in June, the emphasis is on music, but there are plays, ballets and exhibitions.

Hope well and have well.

Ston Easton Park

Ston Easton, near Bath
Telephone: (01761241) 631

The hotel, formerly a Palladian mansion of noted architectural distinction, is set in landscaped grounds not far from Bath. It's easy to see how time can lose all importance as one is seated in the elegant drawing room sipping tea from china cups and silver teapots.

What to see:

A few miles away is Bath, and, northward, such other lovely spots as Corsham, Lacock and the Chippenham-Calne area. Longleat, Dereham Manor and the American Museum at Claverton Manor are within driving distance. The City of Bristol has a long history of maritime adventure and commerce.

Never try to prove what nobody doubts.

THE TEA:

The rich, tasty Sally Lunn bun can be served in several ways – toasted with hot butter, filled with strawberry jam, cream or butters; with a savoury filling it can make a light meal. There are always three or four other cakes that go well with a cup of Indian, China or herbal tea. Price: set tea from £3.50.

OPEN:

Monday to Sunday 10.00am (12.00 Sunday) to 6.00pm. Closed Christmas and New Year.

GETTING THERE:

Bath can be reached on the A4, A36, and A46 roads. Nearest motorway M4. Parking restricted to car parks.

THE TEA:

The tea menu is varied and essentially classic, including scones with clotted cream, Eccles cakes and strawberry tarts, and a good selection of gateaux. There's an interesting selection of teas. Price: from £8.

OPEN:

Monday to Sunday 3.30 to 5.30pm. All through the year.

GETTING THERE:

Ston Easton is on the A37 road. Nearest motorway M4. Own car park.

Copperfields

Woburn
Telephone: (01525) 290464

The lace covered windows, low-beamed ceiling and dark green walls of Copperfields tea room create the right ambience for an assured range of home-made scones and cakes, drawing in crowds of people-locals and visitors alike. This traditional approach to eating and drinking is timeless.

What to see:

Most people come to the area to see Woburn Abbey, home of the Duke of Bedford. It is a mainly 18th-century mansion with outstanding collections of furniture, paintings and ceramics. The Wild Animal Kingdom has a drive-through safari road. The village of Elstow is, perhaps, the county's finest and has many associations with John Bunyan.

THE TEA:
The menu is straightforward and fresh. Light lunches and set teas are served, and a selection of home baked scones, biscuits and cakes can be enjoyed Price: from £3.50.

OPEN:
Daily opening from 10.30am to 6.00pm.

GETTING THERE:
Woburn is on the A4012. Nearest motorway M1. Parking in the village.

Go to your brother's house but not every day.

Rainbows

Bedford Street, Ampthill
Telephone: (01525) 840704

Is it a new age centre pretending to be a tea room, or is it a tea room with new age aspirations? The answer is a little bit of both; certainly, there is no other place in Bedfordshire quite like it. Before you choose your refreshment, tune in to the world of healing crystals, Tibetan meditation and higher consciousness. You'll be a better person for it.

What to see:

Old Warden is an attractive village in its own right, built in a quaint fashion in the 19th century. It contains the Shuttleworth Collection of working historic aeroplanes and the Swiss Garden an early 19th-century romantic garden with pretty vistas. Both are open to the public but check opening times.

THE TEA:
The tea room ladies serve various light snacks and drinks together with a selection of pastries and cakes, mostly home made. Price: from £2.50.

OPEN:
Monday to Friday from 10.00am to 6.00pm. Saturday from 9.00am. Sunday 11-5.00pm.

GETTING THERE:
Ampthill is on the B530 road. Nearest motorway M1. Parking in the town.

Fine words butter no parsnips.

THE TEA:
A cream tea entices with scones, cream and preserve and pots of Earl Grey or Darjeeling. The high tea is also very popular, as are the generous portions of home-made cakes. Price: cream tea £4.

OPEN:
Wednesday to Sunday 11.30am to 5.30pm and some evenings. Closed Monday and Tuesday.

GETTING THERE:
Milton Ernest is just off the A6 north of Bedford. Parking in the village and at the Strawberry Tree.

———◇———
The better the day the better the deed.
———◇———

THE TEA:
The set teas are plain and wholesome: a cream tea, a sandwich tea, or a gateaux tea might be on the menu, served with pots of choice tea. Prices: from £4.

OPEN:
Monday to Sunday 3.00 to 5.00pm for tea.

GETTING THERE:
Windsor is well signposted off the M4 motorway, and can be approached from the A308 or A332. Free parking along the riverside, pay and display car parks in the town.

The Strawberry Tree

Milton Ernest
Telephone: (0123482) 3633

This is an olde worlde place – thatch, whitewash, leaded windows, roses and fruit trees outside; open fireplaces, low beams and pale rose walls within! It was built three hundred years ago as three separate cottages. One was a home, one was a hand laundry and one was the old sweet shop!
What to see:
Visitors are often surprised to discover there is plenty to do and see in Bedfordshire – Woburn Abbey, Whipsnade Zoo, Luton Hoo, Castle Ashby, Wrest Park Gardens, the Dunstable Down.

Berkshire

Drury House

Church Street, Windsor
Telephone: (01753) 863734

This handsome 1600s building, once believed to have been the home of Nell Gwynne, is tucked away on a cobbled street close to Windsor Castle. Beyond the downstairs parlour is a twisting staircase leading up to the tea room. Here you'll find comfortable furniture and elegant, original oak panelling. All visitors seem to enjoy the special atmosphere and sense of history at Drury House.
What to see:
Windsor, with its castle, park and theatre, is well known! Over the bridge is Eton High Street full of antique shops and restaurants. The Thames Valley is best explored by boat!

———◇———
At court everyone for himself.
———◇———

The Tea Cosy

High Street, Sonning-on-Thames
Telephone: (01734) 698178

Tucked away in the delightful olde worlde village of Sonning-on-Thames, the Tea Cosy offers good food throughout the day, in a cosy, welcoming atmosphere. In good weather one can relax in the small cottage garden. The adjoining craft shop is a good place for browsing for special gifts and cards, many handcrafted locally, to suit every occasion and pocket.

What to see:
Sonning-on-Thames is an attractive riverside village, with an 18th-century eleven-arched brick bridge across the Thames. It has Georgian houses and Victorian alms cottages, and beautiful views over the countryside.

THE TEA:
Drop in for a morning snack, lunch or for a clotted cream tea. An appetising selection of home-made cakes, scones and sandwiches, served with steaming pots of tea, are available all day. Price: from £3.

OPEN:
Monday to Saturday 10.00am to 5.00pm, Sunday 1.00 to 5.30pm.

GETTING THERE:
Sonning-on-Thames is three miles north-east of Reading off the A4. Parking is permitted in and around the village.

Life is made up of little things.

The Tutti Pole

3, High Street, Hungerford
Telephone: (01488) 682515

The name 'Tutti' comes from the 'Tithing' or 'Tutti' men who still call in each year to collect a penny from all the Common Right houses and a kiss from the cottage occupants. The men carry a 'Tutti Pole' which is a long staff decorated with flowers, an orange, and some blue ribbon. For many years the staffs were made in the cottage where the tea shop now is.

What to see:
Picturesque Hungerford is well known for its scores of antique and collectors shops. Nearby are the often windswept heights of the Berkshire Downs, where many a racehorse trains, and you can walk along the prehistoric Ridgeway Path. The Kennet valley offers the walker and driver green fertile meadows and birch and oak woods.

THE TEA:
This 'Tutti' is always busy as it offers hot snacks and meals all day. But the staff are friendly and the plump scones with Guernsey cream and a pot of tea are worth waiting for. Price: from £3.50.

OPEN:
Monday to Friday from 9.00am to 5.30pm. Saturday to 6.00pm. Sunday 10.00am to 6.00pm. Closed Christmas and New Year.

GETTING THERE:
Hungerford is on the A4 Nearest motorway M4 Parking in the town

Pleasant hours fly past.

Princess Alexandra

Dear Ms. Cress,

Princess Alexandra has asked me to write and thank you for your letter.

The Princess does not have time for afternoon tea but she likes most teas and is, in fact, a tea drinker.

In hoping that your book will be a success, Her Royal Highness sends her warmest good wishes to you.

Yours Sincerely,
Personal Secretary

Burgers

The Causeway, Marlow
Telephone: (01628) 483389

The Burger family have been baking assorted breads, pastries and chocolates, since the 1940s. The ever-changing array of English and Continental cakes is welcoming. Upstairs is where all the chocolates and pastries are made, while on the main floor, a tea room provides the perfect spot for sampling everything that tempts the palate.

What to see:
Marlow is a pleasant and pretty Georgian town on the banks of the Thames. The peaceful atmosphere can have changed very little since Mary Shelley wrote 'Frankenstein' in a house in West Street, or Jerome K Jerome wrote his quite different classic *Three Men in a Boat* at the Two Brewers tavern in St Peter's Street. Once a year in mid-June there is a Regatta with boat races and a firework display.

THE TEA:
Help yourself to the selection of cakes in the tea room. A special selection of estate teas includes Earl grey, Darjeeling, pure Ceylon and many more. A cream tea is priced at £4.

OPEN:
Monday to Saturday 8.30am to 5.30pm. Closed Sunday.

GETTING THERE:
Marlow is situated on the A404/A4155. Parking is available in and around the town, free and pay and display.

That is well spoken that is well taken.

Chenies Manor

Chenies
Telephone: (01494) 762888

The manor house was the original home of the Russells – Earls and Dukes of Bedford – and was visited by Henry VIII and Elizabeth I. Of particular interest are the Tudor chimneys, the ancient well and the splendid gardens.

What to see:
Chenies is celebrated as a place to visit for the beauty of its gardens. Visitors come from all over the country to see the sunken, white and physic gardens. Tunnels (age uncertain) run underneath the lawns and there is an ancient well. In the flint church the Bedford Chapel has a magnificent collection of funeral monuments. Special permission is required to visit the church.

Patience, time and money accommodate all things.

THE TEA:
Housed in the restored barn, the tea room is simply decorated and furnished. There is a good selection of home-made cakes, with well made cups of tea, served by friendly ladies. Price: from £2.

OPEN:
April to September: Wednesday and Thursday only, 2.00 to 5.00pm. Also Bank Holidays. Entrance fee.

GETTING THERE:
Chenies Manor is off the A404 between Rickmansworth and Chesham. Nearest motorway M25. Own car park.

THE TEA:
The old servants quarters make an unusual and fascinating setting for tea. Home-made cakes, scones and shortbread are served with pots of tea. Price: from £4.

OPEN:
End of March to end of October: Saturday to Wednesday 1.00 to 5.00pm. Closed Thursday and Friday and November to end of March.

GETTING THERE:
Middle Claydon is signposted off the A41 A413 roads. Nearest motorway M1. Own car park.

Time is a great healer.

THE TEA:
A full afternoon tea of sandwiches, scones and pastries is served with the accompaniment of Indian, China and Earl Grey tea. Price: from £11.50.

OPEN:
Daily 3.30 to 5.30pm.

GETTING THERE:
Marlow is on the A4155. Nearest motorways M4, M40 and M25. Hotel car park.

Live well and live forever.

Claydon House

Middle Claydon
Telephone: (01296) 730349

Claydon House has been the home of the Verney family for hundreds of years; the mainly 18th-century house contains a series of fine Rococo state apartments and an unusual Chinese room. A suite of rooms, once occupied by Florence Nightingale (her sister married Sir Harry Verney), is now a museum to her.

What to see:
Buckinghamshire is one of the loveliest counties around London; in the south are the Chiltern Hills, with dense forests of beeches (beautiful at any time of the year); and in the north the Vale of Aylesbury threaded by many little streams.

Compleat Angler Hotel

Marlow Bridge, Marlow
Telephone: (01628) 484444

The hotel takes its name from the famous book by Izaak Walton, written here in 1653. Nowadays, however, the river scene is more to do with pleasure boats than solitary fishermen. An afternoon tea at this picturesque Thames-side hotel offers the additional pleasure of sweeping river views.

What to see:
This charming town, on a pleasant stretch of the Thames with one of the river's finest bridges has much to interest the visitor. It was at Albion House in West Street, that the Shelleys lived for a short period. Mary was working on Frankenstein and Shelley on 'The Revolt of Islam'. The church contains a monument to Sir Miles Hobart who in 1682 locked the door of the House of Commons barring the King's messenger.

The Georgian Coffee House

Wycombe End, Old Beaconsfield
Telephone: (01494) 678550

The Georgian Coffee House nestles close to the crossroads of the town. Inside, it is a simple, no frills place with cream coloured rooms and oak tables and settles. The atmosphere is friendly and relaxed – ideal for a light meal or family tea.

What to see:

The old town of Beaconsfield contains charming shops, and the world's first model village, Bekonscot, built in 1929. The village of Penn has a Norman church and will always be associated with William Penn, leader of the Society of Friends and 'Father of Pennsylvania' in America.

THE TEA:

The simple menu includes a selection of quiches and sandwiches, scones and home-made cakes, as well as a choice of different teas. Prices are very reasonable, from £4.

OPEN:

Monday to Saturday 9.30am to 5.30pm. Closed Sunday.

GETTING THERE:

Beaconsfield can be reached from the M40 (A40) road. Parking is available in the town.

Be as you would seem to be.

Old Jordans

Jordans
Telephone: (0149487) 4586

Down a quiet country lane lies this most delightful house, still a meeting place for Quakers yet open to all as a 'well from which to draw waters of peace'. Inside, 17th-century floors and original furniture still remain, it is quite simply perfect.

What to see:

History has made Jordans renowned, because it is the burial place of William Penn the Quaker, founding father of Pennsylvania, USA. The Mayflower Barn is so named because beams used in the construction are believed to have come from the ship in which the Pilgrim Fathers sailed to America.

THE TEA:

Tea is plain and wholesome, home-made scones and cakes are served with pots of Indian, jasmine or herbal teas. Price: from £2.50.

OPEN:

Daily 3.00 to 5.00pm. Functions are sometimes held at weekends, please phone to check.

GETTING THERE:

Jordans is two miles west of Chalfont St Giles. Nearest main road A40. Nearest motorways M25 and M40. Own car park.

Spread the table and contention will cease.

Stephanie Cole

29 January 1995.

Dear Patricia Rose Cress,

Thank you so much for your letter. I have to admit that coffee or a good single malt are my favourite tipples - however, tea with all the accoutrement, i.e. scones and cream cakes at the Ritz is not to be sneezed at!

Best wishes,

Stephanie Cole.

Stirling Moss Limited

SM/SP

14th December, 1994.

Ms. Patricia Rose Cress,
c/o 91, North End Road,
London, NW11 7TA.

Dear Ms Rose,

Thank you for your letter.

Yes, I do enjoy a cup of tea but now find that it is vying 50/50 with coffee for my attention. This is probably because I go to America a lot and their tea is really awful!

Have a good Christmas.

Yours sincerely,

Stirling Moss

The Myrtle Tree

8 Market Place, Chalfont St Peter
Telephone: (01753) 885371

You could easily pass by the unassuming Myrtle Tree café in the centre of this quiet town – but there is more to it than meets the eye! Even the gift shop within is a little different from the average, selling gifts and books with a religious connection. Tucked away behind all this is a tea room – quietly decorated and simply furnished – many visitors come for the tranquil atmosphere, charming service and home-cooked food.

What to see:
The area is very interesting with beautiful scenery. Milton's cottage is at Chalfont St Giles, as is the Chiltern Open Air Museum, where ancient buildings have been saved from destruction and re-erected.

THE TEA:
The cakes are interesting, with a selection that includes sponges, macaroons, and a variety of chocolate slices. Prices are very reasonable.

OPEN:
Monday to Saturday 9.00am to 5.00pm. Closed Thursday afternoon from 2.00pm and all day Sunday.

GETTING THERE:
Chalfont St Peter is signposted off the A413 Amersham Road. Parking is permitted in the town.

Give and spend, and God will send.

Swanbourne Cottage Tea Rooms

26-28 Winslow Road, Swanbourne
Telephone: (01296) 720516

Swanbourne Cottage used to be the village bakery, and older visitors can still remember running down the lane for a warm, penny loaf! Inside the cottage is as much a cosy tea room as an interesting museum, filled with all kinds of small treasures – pictures, books, lace and china, all of which enhances the old-fashioned tea room atmosphere.

What to see:
Swanbourne is a most interesting village – well worth exploring. Nearby Aylesbury is picturesque threaded with inns, pathways and courtyards, and the village of Long Crendon contains a house that once belonged to Catherine of Aragon.

Nothing is impossible to a willing heart.

THE TEA:
The Swanbourne offers some unusual home-made cakes. Try the Dorset apple cake, or what about a slice of Battenberg? You might prefer to stick to cucumber sandwiches, followed by scones, served with a pot of Lapsang Souchong or rosehip tea. Price: from £3.

OPEN:
Monday to Wednesday 10.00am to 5.00pm, Saturday and Sunday 10.00am to 6.00pm. Closed Thursday and Friday.

GETTING THERE:
Swanbourne is east of Winslow on the B4032. Parking is permitted in the village.

Perfect Setting

All Saints Passage, Cambridge
Telephone: (01223) 354188

Entrance to this delightful tea room is via a shop selling table and bed linen. The atmosphere is pleasant with watercolours on the walls, pine furniture and pretty crockery. Everything is carefully prepared and served by welcoming staff.

What to see:

Cambridge itself takes days to explore but if time is limited, the following should be visited: King's, Trinity, Queen's and Corpus Christi colleges, the Botanic Gardens opened in 1846, and the magnificent art treasures of the Fitzwilliam Museum. On the top of the Gog Magog Hills is an Iron Age hill fort.

*Penny and penny laid up
will be many.*

THE TEA:

The tea menu concentrates on sandwiches made from freshly cut home-made bread, to afternoon teas of scones and appealing cakes. A good choice of teas includes Indian, China and Earl Grey. Price: from £3.

OPEN:

Monday to Saturday 9.30am to 5.30pm. Closed Sunday and Bank Holidays, except summer months.

GETTING THERE:

Cambridge is on the A10 A45 A604 roads. Nearest motorway M11. Town car parks.

Old Bridge Hotel

High Street, Huntingdon
Telephone: (01480) 52681

The Old Bridge is an ivy-clad Georgian hotel, with lawns and gardens running down to the River Ouse. The comfortable and elegant lounge with glass fronted terrace provides a distinctive setting for afternoon tea. Tea is served in the garden in fine weather.

What to see:

Oliver Cromwell was born in the town of Huntingdon in 1599. The grammar school which he and also Samuel Pepys attended is now a museum devoted to Cromwelliana. The town is composed mainly of Georgian buildings, but separating it from Godmanchester is one of the finest medieval bridges in the country, dating from the early 14th century.

Time is, time was, and time is past.

THE TEA:

There is a well chosen assortment of scones, shortbread, fruit tarts, cakes, pastries and fruits in season. There is a fine selection of teas. Price: from £6.

OPEN:

Monday to Sunday 3.00 to 6.00pm. All year round.

GETTING THERE:

Huntingdon is on the A1, A14 and A604 roads. Nearest motorway M11. Own car park.

Steeplegate

16-18 High street, Ely
Telephone: (01353) 664731

Steeplegate is both a tea room and a craft shop. Downstairs, the shop is packed with unusual gifts and handmade goods in pottery, wood, glass and basketware. Upstairs, the tea room is full of character with sloping floors, old windows and wooden tables and chairs.

What to see:

Around the precincts of Ely Cathedral are the houses of the King's School founded by King Henry VII. Close by is the Bishop's Palace and St Mary's Church, in the vicarage of which Oliver Cromwell and his family lived from 1636 to 1647.

In the country I always fear that creation will expire before tea time.
– Sydney Smith

THE TEA:
The tea menu could hardly be simpler – home-made biscuits, teacakes and scones, not to mention cheesecakes and creamy gateaux. The choice of teas includes Indian, fruit and herbal.
Price: set tea from £3.50.

OPEN:
Monday to Saturday 10.00am to 5.00pm. Closed Sunday, Christmas and Bank Holidays.

GETTING THERE:
Ely is on the A10 and A142 roads. Parking is restricted but not difficult.

The Tea Room

East Street, Kimbolton
Telephone: (01480) 860415

Outside are the centuries old, picturesque village houses; inside are tiny rooms, low beams, stone tiled floors, lace tablecloths and bone china, and a delicious display of cakes on the old pine dresser. On fine days tea is served in the garden.

What to see:

Kimbolton has a wide High Street with several interesting old houses, and this runs parallel with East Street, in which the buildings are also of historical interest. Kimbolton Castle (now a school) was the last home of Catherine of Aragon, who died there. It is open to the public at certain times.

Better say here it is than here it was.

THE TEA:
The Tea Room offers home-made cakes such as ginger, Dundee, chocolate and lemon, strawberry and traditional cream teas, as well as a variety of freshly made sandwiches. There is a small choice of teas. Price: from £3.

OPEN:
Tuesday to Sunday 11.00am to 5.00pm. Closed Monday and Christmas and New Year.

GETTING THERE:
Kimbolton is west of Cambridge on the A45. Nearest motorway M11. Parking in the village streets.

THE TEA:

Naturally the menu wouldn't be complete without a clotted cream tea. There may be meringues and tarts, and if you can manage, filling snacks and savouries too. The home-made ice-cream is a must. Price: from £3.

OPEN:

Monday to Sunday from 10.00am to 5.30pm from April to October. 10.30am to 5.00pm November to March.

GETTING THERE:

Tattenhall is signposted off the A41 Chester Road. Nearest motorway M6. Own car park.

You reap what you sow.

THE TEA:

The full afternoon tea is well prepared, with sandwiches, scones and fancy cakes. An added bonus is the delicate choices of tea on the menu. Price: from £9.75.

OPEN:

Daily from 3-5.00pm. Booking advisable at weekends. Closed Christmas.

GETTING THERE:

Chester is on the A41, A49, A55, A59 roads. Nearest motorways M6, M53, M56. Limited parking.

Big is beautiful.

Caroline's Pantry

Cheshire Farm Newton Lane, Tattenhall
Telephone: (01829) 70995

The farm is located just outside the village of Tattenhall on the way to Chester. It is a fully operational dairy farm and the herd of more than three hundred cows can be watched providing one of the main ingredients for afternoon tea. In the meantime, the kettle will already be on the boil in the friendly, next-door pantry.

What to see:

Apart from the city of Chester, Cheshire is a relatively unknown county and there is much to explore. Ancient woodlands, hilltop castles, peaceful villages and small towns have survived unspoilt, and throughout Cheshire there is an extensive canal network, with good scenery and well-maintained towpaths.

Chester Grosvenor

Eastgate Street, Chester
Telephone: (01244) 324024

The Chester is quite a modest affair as hotels go, but handsome, set in the centre of this renowned city. Pass through the front doors, cross the marble-floored lobby and wend your way to the panelled library, a private away-from-it-all spot. Here, nine or ten tables are laid for the service of afternoon tea. The waiting staff are gracious and professional.

What to see:

The city is, of course, of outstanding interest. It is full of beguiling black-and-white houses and other such buildings. One of its most famous assets is the Rows: a series of sets of two-storey shops with open arcaded galleries. Chester's cathedral of red stone dates back to the 14th century and its town wall is more complete than any other in the country.

The Lockside Tea Room

Canal Centre, Hassall Green
Telephone: (01270) 762266

A wonderful spot for recharging the batteries. What could be more idyllic then sipping a drink and watching a cavalcade of colourfully-decorated narrow boats gently gliding by. The tea room is decorated in the traditional colours and patterns associated with canal boats.

What to see:
One of the earliest, and greatest of the man-made waterways was the Trent and Mersey Canal, wending its way from the North to the towns of middle England. A series of locks control the flow of water, including one at Hassall Green. The towpaths offer interesting walks.

THE TEA:
The menu is simplicity itself. There are home-made cakes, pies and meringues or a set cream tea. In summer amble out on to the lawn. Price: from £3.

OPEN:
Daily from 9.30am to 5.00pm. Canal Centre from 8.00am to 6.00pm.

GETTING THERE:
Hassall Green is signposted off the A533. Nearest motorway M6. Car park.

He that follows nature is never out of his way.

Cornwall

Antiques & Teas at Turnpike Cottage

The Square, Gerrans
Telephone: (01872) 580 853

Passers-by often pause here, just to look at this pretty white cottage with its stable door. Beyond the door is a charming, small tea room, offering some excellent Cornish baking. This is a good place for anyone who enjoys tea and collecting, for most of the porcelain, small items and dainty antiques which decorate the room are all for sale.

What to see:
The quiet lanes and villages in this area are delightful to explore. Gerrans is a bright little village on the crest of a hill. Only five minutes away, under the cliffs, is Portscatho, good for bathing. St Mawes is the main town in this area and in the summer is a bustling tourist centre for the verdant Roseland peninsula.

THE TEA:
Apart from the cream teas, the cakes are good – all baked by the owner. If the Cornish Hevva cake is on the menu, go for it! A limited selection of teas is on offer. Price: from £3.

OPEN:
Tuesday to Sunday from 11.00am to 1.00pm and 3.00 to 6.00pm. Easter to end of October. Closed Monday. Winter, open weekends only 3.00 to 6.00pm.

GETTING THERE:
Gerrans is reached via the A3078. Parking is possible.

Little pot is soon hot.

21

THE TEA:

As well as scones and teabreads there are meringues with cream and some very tasty cakes. So save room for chocolate, coconut and whisky slices, served by ladies in long pinnies. Price: from £2.

OPEN:

Monday to Sunday 10.00am to 5.00pm. Closed Christmas and Boxing day.

GETTING THERE:

Falmouth is on the A39 A394 roads. Nearest motorway M5. Town car parks.

A fat kitchen makes a lean will.

THE TEA:

Diets or not, cakes, biscuits and puddings are on the menu. Soups, snacks and light lunches are served all day. A Cornish clotted cream tea is priced from £3.00.

OPEN:

Monday to Sunday from 12.00 to 5.30pm April to October. Closed Friday and winter months.

GETTING THERE:

Cotehele is located off the A388 A390 roads. Nearest motorway M5. Own car park.

Take the goods the gods provide.

De Wynne's

55 Church Street, Falmouth
Telephone: (01326) 319259

After a stroll along the waterfront, why not stop for tea at this traditional style tea shop with bow windows and gas lights. It is attractively and simply furnished with wooden settles and benches, and pleasantly adorned with antique pieces and unusual objects.

What to see:

The long main street of Falmouth contains all the buildings that are of historical interest. Quite unusual is the church dedicated to King Charles the Martyr, one of the few anywhere in the country. Pendennis Castle, built by Henry VIII, is open to the public. In the season, there are boat trips around the Fal estuary.

The Edgcumbe Arms

Cotehele, Saltash
Telephone: (01579) 50024

The very name 'Edgcumbe Arms' probably conjures up smoky images of cramped bars with noisy couples and the strains of "2 double gins and a pint of lager" ringing in you ears. The reality, of course, is completely different and more enjoyable. A table in an intimate room nestling beside the river, and a hearty Cornish cream tea. Could anything be more heavenly?

What to see:

Cotehele House built in the 15th century was the home of the Edgcumbe family for hundreds of years. It contains original furniture, armour and tapestries. The gardens are on several levels and stretch down to the River Tamar. Please check opening times.

Sail Loft

The Harbour, St Michael's Mount
Telephone: (01736) 710748

At high tide you must take the ferry, but at low tide it is possible to walk across the cobbled causeway to St Michael's Mount. A converted boat house houses this restaurant and tea room. The menu is enticing, the setting unusual and the service is cheery and welcoming.

What to see:
The old town of Marazion slopes down to the bay with views of St Michael's Mount and a causeway to the island at low tide. The mount is crowned by a 15th-century castle built around an earlier 11th-century Benedictine monastery. There are guided tours of the castle.

Tregain Tea Room

The Post Office, Portloe
Telephone: (01872) 501252

Portloe is one of those places that takes some effort to get to but is the perfect, romantic hideaway once there. Nothing distracts from the cliffs, the walks and the sea-exciting in a storm. Loving couples are able to take tea in the low beamed cottage, originally three tiny ones, or on the terrace in front.

What to see:
It's the coast that draws people to this part of Cornwall. There are plenty of sheltered little bays and pretty villages. Good for family holidays, good for walkers and for those who love sailing or messing about in boats. Mevagissey is certainly worth a visit, the inner harbour is full of light craft and fishermen still come and go with their catches.

THE TEA:
Enjoy a strong pot of tea along with home-made oatcakes, biscuits, and cakes such as Victoria sponge and of course Cornish cream teas. Price: from £2.50.

OPEN:
Monday to Sunday 10.30am to 4.30pm — weather and tide permitting. Closed from 1 November to the end of March.

GETTING THERE:
St Michael's Mount is approached from the town of Marazion on the A394. Town car parks.

November take flail; let ship no more sail.

THE TEA:
Cream teas, cakes, shortbreads and pastries will help to keep you warm at night. Or plump for snacks and light lunches, all very agreeable. Price: from £3.

OPEN:
Daily from 10.00am to 5.00pm April to end of October. Also some evenings. Closed in winter.

GETTING THERE:
Portloe is signposted off the A3078. Parking in the village.

Stolen kisses are sweetest.

THE TEA:

Light lunches, soups and snacks are served all day in the barn. Afternoons open up with cream teas and home-made cakes and biscuits. Waitress and self-service available. Price from £3.50. After, why not, browse in the art and craft gallery.

OPEN:

1 March to 31 October, Monday to Saturday, 10.30am to 5.30pm. Sunday 1-5.00pm. (tea room from 12.00). Please check winter opening times.

GETTING THERE:

Trelissick is 4 miles South of Truro on the B3289. Car park charge.

A man is known by the company he keeps.

THE TEA:

Toasted teacakes, Jap cakes, scones, fresh cream gateaux share popularity with some fine regional baking. All are worth trying. There's also a nice selection of teas including, Indian, China and herbal. Prices are very reasonable, from £3.

OPEN:

Monday to Saturday 10.00am to 5.30pm. Closed Sunday, except Summer months.

GETTING THERE:

Barnard Castle is on the A67 and A688 roads. Nearest motorway A1(M). Parking in Market Place.

Trelissick Gardens

Feock, Truro
Telephone: (01872) 862090

The beautiful gardens and deciduous woods run down to the River Fal. From the gardens – planted with an abundance of those tender shrubs so characteristic of Cornish gardens – are tantalising views of the water, where all manner of cargo ships can be seen laid up. There is an entrance fee. The mansion is not open to the general public.

What to see:

Truro is Cornwall's only city and the administrative centre of Cornwall. It has dignity, charm and some fine Georgian buildings. The cathedral, begun in 1880, dominates the town. Truro is an excellent shopping centre with all the usual stores and a regular market. St Mawes is an interesting town.

County Durham

Market Place Teashop

29 Market Place, Barnard Castle
Telephone: (01833) 690110

It is worth taking a trip to Barnard Castle for afternoon tea at this quaint tea shop. Old stone walls, flagstone floors, low beams, wooden tables and an open fire on colder days all add to the cosy charm.

What to see:

The town takes its name from the ruined castle founded by Guy de Bailleul in the 12th century. Its best preserved feature is the Round Tower. The Market Cross dates back to 1747, and not far away are Blagraves House (Oliver Cromwell rested here) and The King's Head where Charles Dickens stayed while writing Nicholas Nickleby. Do visit the Bowes Museum – it is an unexpected surprise.

Time and tide wait for no man.

Brownside Coach House

Alston
Telephone: (01434) 381263

Just sitting in the old beamed coach house is a real treat, particularly for city dwellers. On a warm summer's day just sit back and admire the lush greenery of the English countryside whilst sipping a soothing cup of tea.

What to see:
Alston is the highest market town in England, and makes a good centre for touring the sweeping moorlands nearby. West of Alston runs the Pennine Way. Places of interest include Nenthead, the highest village in England, and Hartside Height with panoramic views over the Eden Valley ranging from lakeland fells to Scottish hills.

THE TEA:
A good selection of home-baking offers strawberry gateaux, fresh cream cakes and a very tasty cheesecake. A small range of teas includes Indian and Earl Grey. Price: afternoon tea from £3.

OPEN:
Easter to October: Monday to Sunday 10.00am to 6.00pm. Closed Tuesday and from October to Easter.

GETTING THERE:
Alston is on the A686 and A689 roads. Nearest motorway M6. Ample car parking.

Plain dealing is praised.

Chesters

Kirkstone Galleries, Skelworth Bridge
Telephone: (0153 94) 32553

The A593 out of Ambleside will bring you to the Kirkstone Galleries, where you will discover all kinds of interesting and unusual objects for sale – all fashioned from the local slate. The café/tea room echoes the theme with slate floors, table tops, and slate terraces.

What to see:
The A593 leads to Coniston, amid scenery that is rugged, colourful and punctuated by towering peaks. The village has strong connections with the painter John Ruskin and his house is open to the public. The lake is celebrated for the water speed records of Donald Campbell. The best views are from Tarn Hows, land which was bequeathed by Beatrix Potter, now owned by the National Trust.

He that cannot ask cannot live.

THE TEA:
Throughout the day there is a mouth-watering display of home-baked cakes such as coffee, walnut, and tangy lemon as well as various snacks and savouries. There is a choice of teas. Price: from £2.50.

OPEN:
Monday to Sunday 10.00am to 5.00pm (6.00pm in the summer). Closed Christmas and first week of January.

GETTING THERE:
Take the A593 out of Ambleside. Nearest motorway M6. Own car park.

TOM COURTENAY

Garrick
Theatre

I love my cuppa. Though
I know it is bad for
you. I drink a lot of
Luaka tea — low in
tannin and not so
bad for you!

T.C.

Dent Crafts Centre

Dent, Helmside
Telephone: (015396) 25400

There are at least two reasons to visit this lovely, well stocked craft centre. One reason, of course, is the imaginative selection of craftwork on sale. The other is to enjoy an excellent cup of tea and some good, flavoursome home-baking.

What to see:

The old town of Dent has a narrow cobbled main street lined with grey and white stone cottages. It has an unhurried, unchanging atmosphere and long may it remain so. Close to the church is a memorial to Alan Sedgwick, the noted Victorian geologist.

THE TEA:

The tea menu offers a small selection of home-baked cakes as well as some quite wonderful wholemeal scones. There is a choice of Indian, China and herbal teas. Price: from £2.50.

OPEN:

Monday to Sunday 9 30am to 5.30pm. Closed weekdays January to early March.

GETTING THERE:

Dent is off the A683 and A684 roads. The drive is particularly scenic. Nearest motorway M6. Own car park.

There is no love sincerer than the love of food.
– George Bernard Shaw

The Dove Cottage Tea Shop

Town End, Grasmere
Telephone: (015394) 35544

At Town End is Dove Cottage, the home of Wordsworth where he lived with his sister, Dorothy, and then later his bride, Mary. It is preserved almost as it was when they lived there. The attractive beamed tea room – part of Dove Cottage and the Wordsworth Museum, serves afternoon tea in a charming lounge with comfortable armchairs and settees.

What to see:

The area around the lake and village is noted for its beauty. Coleridge wrote, 'We drank tea the night before I left Grasmere on the island in that lovely lake, our kettle swung over the fire, hanging from the branch of a fir tree'. It is a wonderous area to explore on foot.

Old customs are best.

THE TEA:

The tea menu offers a good choice of open sandwiches, together with scones, fruitcake, teabreads and gateaux. Darjeeling, Assam, Earl Grey and herbal teas are available. Price: from £3.

OPEN:

Monday to Sunday 10.00am to 5.30pm. Closed from the middle of January to the middle of February.

GETTING THERE:

Grasmere is on the A591. Nearest motorway M6. Town car parks.

THE TEA:

The secret is simple, a pot of choice tea accompanied by home-baked scones, favourite assorted cakes and pastries such as gingerbread, fruit slices and oatmeal ginger cake with cream or rum butter. Price: from £3.

OPEN:

Tuesday to Sunday 10.30am to 5.00pm. Closed Monday and Christmas. Open weekends only in January.

GETTING THERE:

Hawkshead is on the B5285 and B5286 roads. Nearest motorway M6. Village car park.

---◇---

An occasion lost cannot be redeemed.

---◇---

THE TEA:

Afternoon tea comprises the lightest of scones, served with cream and fresh fruit shortbread, and an irresistible selection of cakes. All this, with excellent tea served in Wedgwood china. Price: set tea from £8 plus service charge.

OPEN:

Monday to Sunday 3.00 to 5.00pm. Closed December until March. Booking advisable.

GETTING THERE:

Windermere is on the A591 and A592 roads. Nearest motorway M6. Parking at the hotel.

Grandy Nook Tea Room

Vicarage Lane, Hawkshead
Telephone: (015394 36) 404

The baking is traditional and excellent, the service cheerful and the atmosphere delightfully rustic at this very popular, tiny tea room in the village of Hawkshead.

What to see:

This charming village, with old cottages, curious alleyways and little courtyards merits a leisurely visit. Wordsworth attended school here and you can see the desk on which he carved his name. The church was built in the 15th century and the medieval courthouse is now a museum. There are beautiful walks and trails to follow in Grizedale Forest.

---◇---

Miller Howe Hotel

Rayrigg Road, Windermere
Telephone: (015394) 42536

A gourmet's delight this celebrated lakeland hotel provides a delectable afternoon tea. From the antique-filled lounges where tea is served, there are sensational views across Windermere to the Cumbrian fells. On fine days tea can be taken on the terrace.

What to see:

Windermere is the largest lake in England as well as the most famous in the Lake District. The steamers that transport holiday makers are an admirable way of seeing the area. If driving, the A591 is the most popular way of entering the Lake District.

---◇---

Tea how I tremble at thy fatal stream As lethe dreadful to the love of fame. – Young

---◇---

Rothay Manor

Rothay Bridge, Ambleside
Telephone: (0153 94) 33605

On a hot summer afternoon this is the sort of place we all want to seek out – a traditional, stylish country house hotel with a beautiful garden and a friendly informal welcome.

What to see:

Ambleside is a busy bustling town and one of the main tourist centres of the Lake district. Within walking distance are the lakes of Windermere, Grasmere and Rydal Water. All around are scenic walks with magnificent views of lakes and fells. In August the internationally famous sheep dog trials are held in Rydal Park.

Content is the philosopher's stone, that turns all it touches into gold.

Sharrow Bay Hotel

Pooley Bridge, near Penrith
Telephone: (017684) 86301

This exquisite hotel enjoys a unique position on the shores of Lake Ullswater, with panoramic views over the lake and surrounding countryside. The elegant lounge or conservatory provide perfect settings for afternoon tea.

What to see:

Pooley Bridge is a good starting point for exploring the area around Ullswater. Dalemain is a fine medieval and Tudor house open to the public. There are also Countryside museums in the area.

None can guess the jewel by the casket.

THE TEA:
Afternoon tea is an excellent buffet of superb cakes and tasty savouries There are old fashioned tarts, spiced fruit cakes, assorted teabreads, cream gateaux, Bara Brith and much more besides. Everything is home-made, and served with a fine choice of teas. Price: from £7.50.

OPEN:
Monday to Sunday 2.45 to 5.30pm. Closed early January to beginning of February.

GETTING THERE:
Ambleside is on the A591 road. Nearest motorway M6. Own car park.

THE TEA:
Knowledgeable visitors of this hotel's marvellous cuisine will be well acquainted with the set afternoon tea of dainty sandwiches, a choice of buttery scones and various melt-in-the-mouth pastries and cakes. A choice of teas includes all the old favourites. Price: £11.25 per person, booking is essential.

OPEN:
March to November only: Monday to Sunday 4.00 to 5.00pm.

GETTING THERE:
Pooley Bridge is on the A592 and B5320 roads. Nearest motorway M6. Limited car parking.

THE TEA:

The tea menu offers a wide range of mouthwatering cakes and breads including spicy Bara Brith, rum flavoured Sachertorte and fresh muffins made with flour ground at Muncaster Mill in Eskdale. Tea blends available include Assam and Darjeeling. Prices are very reasonable, from £3.50.

OPEN:

Monday to Saturday 10.30am to 5.00pm. Closed Sunday and the month of January.

GETTING THERE:

Ambleside is four miles north of Windermere on the A591. Parking in the town.

Speak fitly or be silent wisely.

THE TEA:

The food is astonishingly varied and wholesome. Home-made puddings, cakes and pies are all truly scrumptious served with interesting choices of tea. Price: from £3.

OPEN:

Daily from 10.30am to 5.30pm. Winter open weekends only November-March. Closed January and February.

GETTING THERE:

Dent is off the A683, A684 roads. Nearest motorway M6. Parking in the village..

Sheila's Cottage

The Slack, Ambleside
Telephone: (015394) 33079

This charming 17th-century lakeland stone cottage and adjoining barn, is always busy with a mixture of visitors to the lakes and regular local customers. The setting, wonderfully home-baked food and friendly atmosphere make it a special treat.

What to see:

The town has many literary associations. The Wordsworths lived nearby and the parish church has a commemorative chapel with memorial windows and a bible given by Mrs Wordsworth.

Stone Close

Main Street, Dent
Telephone: (015396) 25231

Stone Close is popular with locals, writers, walkers, and talkers – in fact with any and everyone who chances upon this convivial seventeenth-century cottage still blessed with cast-iron ranges. Some travellers eat three meals a day-the cooking is so tasty, and have been known to stay the night as well. And the next . . . and the next . . .

What to see:

The village-known-locally as Dent Town-has narrow cobbled streets flanked by small cottages roofed with the local stone. The church was founded in the 11th century and has been added to over the centuries. There are many sign posted footpaths that can be followed in the area. It is an easy drive to the lakes, and you can design your own tours.

Be as you would seem to be.

The Village Bakery

Melmerby, Penrith
Telephone: (01768) 881515

The Village Bakery is housed in a converted barn, and exposed beams, old stone walls and flagstones enhance the rustic charm. At the 'bakery' the emphasis is on healthy eating – organic wholemeal flour and home-grown fruit and vegetables are used in the recipes.

What to see:

The village of Melmerby lies in some of the most remote English countryside, and the drive from Penrith to Alston on the A686 follows a particularly attractive route. Of interest in the area is the monolith and stone circle known as 'Long Meg and her daughters'

THE TEA:

A marvellous variety of baked goodies includes carrot cake, Cumberland Rum Nicky, spice cake, Borrowdale teabread and many more. There is a good range of teas. Price: from £3.

OPEN:

Monday to Sunday 8.30am to 5.00pm. January and February 8.30am to 2.30pm. Closed Christmas.

GETTING THERE:

Melmerby is halfway between Penrith and Alston on the A686. Nearest motorway M6. Own car park.

Hunger is the best sauce in the world.
– Miguel Cervantes

The Wild Strawberry

54 Main Street, Keswick
Telephone: (0176 87) 74399

A cheery unpretentious tea room with a traditional feel – old beams, stone walls and flagstone floors. It takes its name from the attractive porcelain which has a colourful strawberry motif. Don't miss the scones – claimed to be the best in the area.

What to see:

Keswick with many literary associations, nestles in a beautiful position below the peak of Skiddaw. It is a popular centre for walking and climbing. Two miles east of the town is the ancient Castlerigg Stone Circle. From this prehistoric site there are beautiful views of the surrounding countryside.

A handful of good life is better than a bushel of learning.

THE TEA:

There is a good range of sandwiches, Home-made cakes and a Cumbrian sweet known as sticky toffee pudding. Tea choices include Indian, China, fruit and herbal. Price: from £3.

OPEN:

Monday to Sunday 10.00am to 5.00pm. Closed Wednesday, two weeks January and all of February.

GETTING THERE:

Keswick is on the A66 A591 roads. Nearest motorway M6. Pay and display car parks.

THE TEA:

This attractive tea room was once the sawmill. Everything is home-made and tea time brings freshly baked scones and a choice of tempting cakes served with a selection of teas. Price: from £2.50

OPEN:

Easter to October: Sunday to Saturday 11.00am to 5.00pm. Closed Monday. Open October to Easter weekends only.

GETTING THERE:

Embleton is east of Cockermouth on the A66. Nearest motorway M6. Own car park.

Wythop Mill

Embleton, near Cockermouth
Telephone: (0176 87) 76394

The mill's water wheel is still driven each day by the fast flowing river beside which it stands. Here you will find a display of old woodworking and wheelwrighting tools and it makes an unusual and interesting stop for tea.

What to see:

The nearby town of Cockermouth is Wordsworth's birthplace, and the house where he was born is open to the public. The town was also the birthplace of Fletcher Christian, leader of the Mutiny on the Bounty. In 1568 Mary Queen of Scots visited the area after fleeing the Battle of Langside.

*One grain fill not a sack,
but helps his fellow.*

THE TEA:

The baking is guaranteed to please the palate. Fruit cakes, Yorkshire parkin and apple pie are just some of the delights on the menu. Everything is available all day. Price: from £2.50.

OPEN:

Monday to Sunday from 10.00am to 6.00pm, winter 5.00pm. Closed Tuesday and 1 week November.

GETTING THERE:

Sedbergh is on the A683 A684 roads. Nearest motorway M6. Parking in the town.

Time is a great healer.

Ye Olde Copper Kettle

43 Main Street, Sedbergh
Telephone: (015396) 20995

This is the kind of tea room you'd want in any town-inviting, friendly, a place to sip and chat. Not surprising then that it is very popular – good food, like good news, travels fast. The setting is a tiny, cottagey tea room in the cobbled main street of the old town of Sedbergh.

What to see:

The narrow main street was part of the turnpike between Kendal and Kirkby Stephen. Note the charming 17th-century Friends' meeting house, where George Fox, the founder of the society is said to have preached. Nearby Kirkby Stephen is worth visiting for its antique shops and interesting medieval church.

Caudwell's Mill

Rowsley, near Bakewell
Telephone: (01629) 733185

Caudwell's Mill, built in the 19th century, is a complex of craft workshops and a working water-powered mill where you can take tea while enjoying the lovely view. Everything is made on the premises using the freshly milled flour.

What to see:
The village is at the meeting point of the Rivers Wye and Derwent and on the edge of the Chatsworth and Haddon estates. It is well placed for touring either the dramatic 'Dark Peak' or the gentler 'White Peak' regions of Derbyshire. It is a wonderful county to explore, some of its best parts can still only be reached on foot.

He that would know what shall be, must consider what has been.

Chatsworth

Near Bakewell
Telephone: (01246) 582204

Hundreds of thousands of visitors come to see Chatsworth House, its gardens and its park every year – and of course the wonderful tea room. It was formed from the old stables, each stall still labelled with the name of a horse, but now well carpeted!

What to see:
Chatsworth has been open to the public since it was built in the late 17th century by 'Bess of Hardwick' and her second husband Sir William Cavendish. The house contains a superb collection of furnishings, furniture and works of art. The garden has a fine cascade and one of the highest fountains in Europe. Please check opening times.

He that goes far, has many encounters.

THE TEA:
At tea time there is a good selection of wholemeal cakes, like cinnamon and apricot slice, flapjacks or banana and walnut loaf. There is a wide range of herbal teas. Price: from £2.50.

OPEN:
October to March: Monday to Sunday 10.00am to 6.00pm. January and February: weekends only, 10.00am to 4.00pm.

GETTING THERE:
Rowsley is on the A6. Nearest motorway M1. Own car park.

THE TEA:
Luxurious chocolate cake, butter shortbread and scones served with freshly made raspberry jam are very tempting. The choice of teas is also excellent. The quality of the food, prepared and baked on the premises is outstanding. Prices are very reasonable, from £3.

OPEN:
Easter to the last week in October: Monday to Sunday 11.00am to 4.30pm.

GETTING THERE:
Chatsworth is north of Matlock off the B6012. Ample parking space.

David Gower

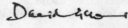

TEA

What would a game of cricket be without a cup of tea in the afternoon?

Just imagine it — Australia 460 for 5 at ten past four on the second day of the Lord's test: time for a cup of tea and one of Nancy's sandwiches.

The trouble is that the tea break is never long enough, but at least after the next couple of hours the boys can look forward to something even stronger!

David Gower

Cottage Tea Room

Fennel Street, Ashford-in-the-Water
Telephone: (01629) 812488

The 'Cottage' typifies the delights of having tea in a village setting. The decor is simple and refreshing, the service is friendly and attentive, and the home-baking is a satisfying discovery.

What to see:
Three bridges span the River Wye in this pretty village. The oldest is the Sheepwash Bridge standing exactly as it was constructed over three-hundred years ago. The church, though rebuilt, dates originally from Norman times. At Fin Cop, one and a half miles north-west of the village, are the remains of an Iron Age fort.

I eat well, and I drink well,
and I sleep well – but that's all.
Thomas Morton

THE TEA:
Set teas feature lovely scones, teabreads and cakes such as carrot and honey, all served with an excellent pot of tea. Everything is home-made and additive-free. Price: from £3.

OPEN:
Monday to Wednesday 10.30am to 12.00 noon and 2.30 to 5.00pm, Thursday 2.30 to 5.00pm, Saturday and Sunday 10.00am to 12 noon and 2.30 to 5.00pm. Closed Christmas and New Year.

GETTING THERE:
Ashford-in-the-Water is on the A6. Nearest motorway M1. Village car park.

Eyam Tea Rooms

The Square, Eyam
Telephone: (014336) 31274

In one of Derbyshire's most famous villages – in 1665 the inhabitants stayed within the parish confines and so prevented the plague from spreading elsewhere – is a very popular tea room. Warmth and character are all around as well as a real sense of history, the house dates from 1650.

What to see:
Many visitors to the area come simply for the scenery and the glorious walks; but there are plenty of towns and villages (some with summer 'well dressing' ceremonies) worth visiting as well as old churches, and stately homes to explore.

In the coldest flint there is hot fire.

THE TEA:
Tea might include freshly made sandwiches, lovely light scones with jam and cream, airy sponges and moist fruit cake. There is a choice of up to twenty speciality teas and infusions. Price: from £3.50.

OPEN:
February to October: Tuesday to Sunday 10.30am to 6.00pm. Closed Mondays and November to February.

GETTING THERE:
Eyam is signposted off the A623 road. Nearest motorway M1. Parking in the village.

THE TEA:
There is a good selection of scones, tarts, biscuits as well as superb cakes and gateaux, all made on the premises. A range of teas includes Indian, China and herbal. Price: from £3.

OPEN:
Monday to Saturday 8.30am to 5.00pm. Closed Sunday January and February, check opening times.

GETTING THERE:
Ashbourne is on the A52, A515 and A517 roads. Nearest motorway M1. Town car parks.

Gingerbread Shop

26 St John Street, Ashbourne
Telephone: (01335) 346753

A great favourite with locals and visitors alike, this cheerful combination of tea room and bakery in the centre of town offers remarkable cakes, tarts and of course, gingerbread men.

What to see:
The town of Ashbourne is renowned for: Church Street, its main street, unchanged since the time of Charles I, its fine interesting church and a food, gingerbread. The recipe came from the captured French soldiers billeted here during the Napoleonic Wars and has been baked ever since, the recipe passed from baker to baker down the years.

When going to an eating house go to one that is filled with customers.

THE TEA:
Look out for the daily-changing home-baked goodies. There might be melt-in-your-mouth shortbread, scrumptious chocolate cake and classic Bakewell tart. A good choice of herbal, fruit as well as Indian teas. Price: from £3.50.

OPEN:
Tuesday to Saturday 9.00am to 5.00pm.

GETTING THERE:
Hope is east of Sheffield on the A625. Nearest motorway M1. Parking in the village.

Hopechest

8 Castleton Road, Hope, near Sheffield
Telephone: (014336) 20072

Take a break while visiting the Hope Valley and go to this friendly cottagey tearoom at the back of a wholefood and craft shop. On warm days have tea in the pretty walled garden.
Closed Monday (except Bank Holidays) and Sunday, Christmas and New Year.

What to see:
Many visitors come here for the scenery and glorious walks, the Pennine Way starts in the Peak District. In Hope itself there is a traditional summer 'well dressing' ceremony and an agricultural show famous for its sheepdog trials.

Sit down and feed and welcome to our table.
– William Shakespeare

Rose Cottage Café

Castleton
Telephone: (014336) 20472

A friendly welcome awaits you at the Rose Cottage Café in the picturesque Hope Valley. They are used to hungry walkers and climbers dropping in and provide all kinds of delicious home-cooking to sample inside, or to take into the pretty rustic garden.

What to see:
The whole area is fascinating and steeped in history. The first thing any visitor sees are the ruins of Peveril Castle, built in William the Conqueror's time and immortalised in Sir Walter Scott's book 'Peveril of the Peak'. This is also the land of caves and caverns and Blue John stone, found nowhere else in the world except here.

THE TEA:
Traditional teatime fare is served in the shape of moist, crumbly scones and delicious cakes and slices. There is a choice of teas. Price: from £3.

OPEN:
Monday to Sunday 10.00am to 5.00pm. Closed Friday, Christmas and all of January.

GETTING THERE:
Castleton is on the A626. Nearest motorway M1. Village car park.

*Kissing don't last,
cookery do!
– George Meredith*

Devon

Buckfast Abbey

Buckfastleigh
Telephone: (01364) 643301

The Abbey, begun in 1907, is a modern rebuilding on the site of a pre-conquest abbey. It was the almost unaided work of six Benedictine monks and took 30 years to complete. There is much to see and admire, however, the monks not only contemplate spiritual nourishment but also cater for our more earthly appetites in their restaurant and tea rooms.

What to see:
From the town of Buckfastleigh it is easy to drive to Torquay and its sandy bays, promenades, colourful gardens and various family attractions, Dartmoor, the River Dart (with several river boat trips), Paignton, Exeter and Plymouth. There are many interesting villages and picturesque fishing ports on the south coast of Devon best seen in spring and autumn.

THE TEA:
The Grange offers home-made snacks, cakes, pies and pastries and several praiseworthy variations of a Devon Cream Tea. The Buckfast Wine Cake is a real tonic and very popular. Price: from £3.

OPEN:
Daily, all year round from 10.00am to 5.30pm. Closes at 4.00pm winter months. Closed Christmas.

GETTING THERE:
Buckfastleigh is on the A38. Nearest motorway M5. Parking in the grounds.

God helps those who help themselves.

THE TEA:
Turn up and enjoy one of the set teas such as: the King's Ransom, a grilled stilton-covered tea cake, or the Seafarer's tea with smoked mackerel. Both go perfectly with one of the fragrant teas. Price: from £3.50.

OPEN:
Monday to Saturday from 9.30 am to 5.30pm. Mondays and Saturdays from 10.00am. Closed Sunday and Wednesday afternoon.

GETTING THERE:
South Molton is on the A361. Nearest motorway M5. Parking in the town.

Time is the father of truth.

THE TEA:
The menu deals in light snacks, hot dishes, sandwiches and home-made cakes and everything is available at any time. Very popular is the Devon Cream Tea. Price: from £3.

OPEN:
Monday to Sunday from 10.00am to 5.00pm. Closed Wednesday. In winter closed Tuesday and Wednesday.

GETTING THERE:
Budleigh Salterton is on the B3178 B3179 roads. Nearest motorway M5. Restricted parking in the town.

Corn Dolly

East Street, South Molton
No Telephone

The thoroughly quaint little Corn Dolly keeps its customers happy by offering excellent home baking, with a commendable reliance on free-range eggs and local produce. At all times, in all seasons, the tea room is friendly and intimate and the food special enough to draw visitors from far and wide. Next door is a craft and gift shop.

What to see:
If you enjoy browsing in antique shops and small markets then South Molton has plenty on offer. Good sandy beaches lie beyond, at Woolacombe, Saunton and Croyde which overlook Barnstaple bay and have National Trust landscape behind them. The nature reserve of Braunton Burrows is unusual and worth a visit.

The Cosy Teapot

Fore Street, Budleigh Salterton
Telephone: (01395) 444016

"Oh, it looks so cosy let's go in" said the mother to the daughter! And so it does. And so should you. Enter a room decorated with interesting prints and pictures and an unusual collection of teapots. Tables are covered with lace cloths, tea is served from bone china and the young serving girls wear floral print pinafores.

What to see:
The town's name derives from the salt pans that used to prosper at the mouth of the river Otter before it silted up in the 15th century. Early in the 19th century it became a fashionable seaside resort for members of the 'genteel' classes and their families. Near by, East Budleigh is a typical, neat Devon village.

Better a small fish than an empty dish.

Four and Twenty Blackbirds

Tea Shoppe 43 Gold Street, Tiverton
Telephone: (01884) 257055

Old tables and chairs of different shapes and sizes, some more antique than others, make the adjoining beamed rooms individual and inviting. There are fresh flowers on the table, and current issues of local and national magazines are on the windowsill and centre table, for visitors to browse through.

What to see:
Tiverton has a good number of fine buildings to discover. The church of St Peter has a well carved chapel and an outstanding organ, it is claimed Mendelssohn's 'Wedding March' was first played here. Blundell's school, founded in 1604, had some noteworthy pupils including RD Blackmore, author of *Lorna Doone*.

THE TEA:
Delights include indulgences served from the trolley, a variety of set teas and assorted sandwiches, teabreads and cakes. The tea blends are also excellent and include Indian and Earl Grey. Prices are very reasonable, from £3.

OPEN:
Monday to Saturday 9.30am to 5.30pm. Closed Sunday.

GETTING THERE:
Tiverton is on the A361 and A396 roads. Nearest motorway M5. Public car parks.

I shall sit here serving tea to friends . . .
– TS Eliot

Georgian Tea Rooms

High Street, Topsham
Telephone: (01392) 873465

If you want to eat at reasonable prices in unpretentious, no frills surroundings and still find yourself enjoying the food, try the Georgian Tea Room. The atmosphere is genuine, much like having tea at a favourite aunt's. Tables are covered with attractive embroidered cloths and plants are dotted about the place.

What to see:
Some of Devon's more unusual sights include Morwellham Quay, a thriving open-air museum in charming countryside, complete with costumed inhabitants; a maritime museum at Exeter, bird gardens, the Dartington glassworks, Bickleigh Mill farm, steam railways, watermills, vintage car collections and any number of mansions and castles.

THE TEA:
Pastries and cakes are light and plentiful. Scones come piping hot and with home-made jam. Also available are light snacks, salads and sandwiches, all choice nibbles. Price: from £2.50.

OPEN:
Monday to Saturday from 9.30am to 5.00pm. Closed on Sundays and the Christmas period.

GETTING THERE:
Topsham is on the A376. Nearest motorway M5. Parking in the town.

If it isn't broken don't fix it.

THE TEA:

A warming pot of tea and a slice of chocolate roulade will help you put on a happy face. There are plenty of other goodies and 20 different kinds of cake to enjoy with 38 excellent choices of tea. Price: from £3.50.

OPEN:

Tuesday to Saturday from 10.00am to 5.00pm. Sunday from 11.30am to 5.00pm. Closed Monday and Wednesday.

GETTING THERE:

Totnes is on the A381 A385 roads. Nearest motorway M5. Parking in the town.

Birds in their little nests agree.

THE TEA:

Food here is tasty, simple, inexpensive and, what's more, smells so good. You can order snacks and sandwiches, enjoy a cream tea or sample one of the 'squidgy cakes'. It goes without saying that Honeybees has a good line of teas. Price: from £2.75.

OPEN:

Monday to Saturday from 10.00am to 5.00pm. Closed on Sunday.

GETTING THERE:

Honiton is on the A30 road. Nearest motorway M5. Parking in the town.

Greys Dining Room

High Street, Totnes
Telephone: (01803) 866369

Outside the setting is a narrow, winding street lined with a variety of little shops. Inside visitors are captivated by the cultured mood of this Georgian house full of good antiques and many other little, personal touches. It is just the place to escape, for a while anyway, the cares and snares of modern day living.

What to see:

The ruins of a Norman castle still dominate the winding, steep streets of this busy market town and the Guildhall and church are of special interest. The boat trips that run from Totnes to Dartmouth are very bracing and a little further away is Widecombe-in-the-Moor with its renowned church and its September fair.

Honeybees

High Street, Honiton
Telephone: (01404) 43392

Honey bees is a comfortable sort of joint, as people like to say. The front room is filled with an informal assortment of wooden tables and mismatched chairs. In the back there's a clutter of crafts to quibble over whilst refuelling. The atmosphere is casual and attracts a friendly, local following.

What to see:

Lace is still made in Honiton, though not on the scale which made it famous a century ago. From here it is but a short drive to old-fashioned seaside resorts such as, Budleigh Salterton, Exmouth and Sidmouth. And inland there are interesting villages, country parks and historic buildings to be explored.

Every bee's honey is sweet..

The Kettle

15 Fore Street, Seaton
Telephone: (01297) 20428

If you are a lover of old, traditional tearooms, you should make a point of calling at 'The Kettle' in the neat, bright town of Seaton. The house is just over 400-years old and retains much of its original character. The atmosphere is convivial and the home baking of a good standard.

What to see:
This is a good base from which to visit the old-fashioned, familiar resorts of Exmouth, Sidmouth and Budleigh Salterton. Inland are pretty villages, country parks and historic buildings such as Forde Abbey or Powderham Castle. Seaton is itself an attractive seaside town.

A rolling eye, a roving heart.

Mearsdon Manor Galleries

Moretonhampstead
Telephone: (01647) 40483

Above the gentle hum of customers eating and drinking contentedly, a familiar cry goes up 'another cream tea please.' A plate piled high with scones is rushed to the table. In the oldest house in town the combining of a gallery, stuffed with Eastern treasures and a traditional English tea room, is rather successful.

What to see:
The Dartmoor National Park attracts people touring by car, anglers, riders, golfers and-above-all-walkers. The town of Moreton merits a lingering visit to explore its streets, houses, and the church of St. Andrew. From here it is easy to motor to Exeter and the south coast.

THE TEA:
Visitors are offered a choice of set teas including scones and perhaps a traditional cake like chocolate or coffee and walnut. A good range of teas is brewed in attractive, china teapots. Price: from £3.

OPEN:
Monday to Sunday from 10.00am to 6.00pm throughout the year. Closed for the month of January.

GETTING THERE:
Seaton is signposted off the A3052. Nearest motorway M5. Parking is possible.

THE TEA:
The menu covers familiar territory, cream teas naturally, and unfussy home-made cakes and scones no one wants to miss. There's a choice of at least 10 different teas. Price: from £3.

OPEN:
Monday to Saturday from 10.00am to 5.00pm. Closed Sunday except afternoons in summer.

GETTING THERE:
Moretonhampstead is on the A382. Nearest motorway M5. Parking in the town.

A cat may look at a king.

Dear Patricia Cress,

 Thank you for your letter and my
apologies for the delay in this reply.

You are quite right in assuming that I adore a cup
of tea. My favourite is undoubtedly Kenya tea.
This is because I went on safari in Kenya a few
years ago, when I tasted it for the first time. I
have been drinking it ever since. I think I can
say that I drink more tea than any other beverage,
or alcohol for that matter! I try to find an
excuse as many times as I can during the day to
partake of one.

Hope this might be of use to you in your book.

With best wishes,

Sincerely yours,

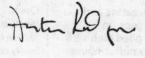

The Mulberry Room

1 Scarborough Road, Torquay
Telephone: (01803) 213639

Settled in at this quiet, prettily furnished tea room, you would never imagine you were just a few minutes away from the bustle of the sea-front. The menu varies according to the seasons, but the 'cake table' is always laden with tasty home-made goodies. To accompany, there's an excellent pot of tea.

What to see:
An elegant, sophisticated seaside resort noted for its sub-tropical shrubs. There is plenty to do; walking, swimming, sailing and riding, as well as to see; art galleries, a museum and Kents Cavern containing stalagmites, stalactites as well as pre-historic human and animal bones.

THE TEA:
The choice is really good, fresh cream meringues, chocolate cakes, fruit slices and a choice of scones. Price: from £3.50.

OPEN:
Wednesday to Sunday 10.00am to 5.00pm. Closed Monday and Tuesday.

GETTING THERE:
Torquay is on the A379. Nearest motorway M5. Street parking and town car parks.

> *When Mr Apollinax visited the USA 'his laughter tinkled among the teacups'.*
> *– TS Eliot*

The Old Clockhouse

Sidbury, near Sidmouth
Telephone: (01395) 597322

Mellow, comfortable and with a most attractive situation in the centre of the village, the Old Clockhouse is open to all who love the unhurried and unchanging atmosphere of a traditional tea room. The aromas of home baking, the tick-tocking of old clocks, the sounds of contented voices – all blend to paint a backcloth of contentment in which this centuries old cottage has pride of place.

What to see:
The village has grown up around the spired church of St Giles, thought to be one of the most interesting in Devon. A Saxon crypt was found under the chancel in 1898. It is one of only half a dozen in the country.

THE TEA:
Teatime treats include a selection of cakes, as well as scones and gingerbread. The scones are served with clotted cream. A selection of teas includes Indian, China and herbal. Price: from £3.

OPEN:
Summer, Tuesday to Sunday 10.30am to 5.00pm. Closed Monday. Winter, open weekends only.

GETTING THERE:
Sidbury is three miles out of Sidmouth on the A375. Nearest motorway M5. Village car park.

Good is good, but better carries it.

THE TEA:
As well as two set teas, the menu maintains a good selection of snacks, salads and sandwiches, tucked in with a small range of home-made cakes. The tea choices are very acceptable. Price: from £3.50.

OPEN:
Monday to Saturday from 10.00am to 5.00pm. Closed Sundays.

GETTING THERE:
Exmouth is on the A376. Nearest motorway M5. Parking in the town.

Two's company three is none.

THE TEA:
The tea menu offers an astonishing selection of pastries and cakes. Try resisting the cheesecakes and meringues or the fruit sponges and eclairs! The clotted cream tea comes with various choices of scones as well as teas. Prices are very reasonable, from £3.

OPEN:
Summer time: Monday to Sunday 10.00am to 5.30pm. Closed September to March.

GETTING THERE:
Lustleigh is just off the A382. Nearest motorway M5. Parking in the village.

Past Times

High Street, Exmouth
Telephone: (01395) 269306

This unashamedly 'Victorian Age' tea room in the High street turns its back on modern manners and uniformity. Instead it offers a genuine welcome, honest food and plenty of it. On fairweather days enjoy tea in the garden or, stretch out your legs on the rattan chairs by the beckoning, open french windows.

What to see:
The town of Exmouth has a sandy beach, good for a family holiday, and a little harbour for small sail boats and light craft. Ferries cross the River Exe to Starcross. Three other traditional seaside towns are: Seaton, Budleigh Salterton and Sidmouth. One of the prettiest places on the coast is Branscombe.

Primrose Cottage

Lustleigh
Telephone: (016477) 365

After a stroll through the village of Lustleigh, stop for tea at this appealing, thatched cottage. Here you'll find genuine hospitality coupled with superb home-baking. If the weather is good pick a table in the tea garden, which leads down to the river.

What to see:
Lustleigh has an interesting history, there are prehistoric remains, King Alfred gave the village to his youngest son and the church dates from the 15th century. West of the village is Lustleigh Cleave, one of Devon's most romantic views.

Memory is the treasury and guardian of all things.
– Cicero

Royal Clarence Hotel

Cathedral Yard, Exeter
Telephone: (01392) 58464

Overlooking the imposing Exeter Cathedral, and spectacularly floodlit at night, the Royal Clarence Hotel lays claim to being the first inn in the country to warrant the title 'Hotel'. Discreetly modernised, the hotel covets its history, with oak panelling, moulded friezes and period furniture.

What to see:

The Cathedral dates, mostly, from the 14th century and is one of England's most beautiful buildings. The city offers a rich variety of architecture – medieval, Regency and modern, the last named due to heavy bombing in 1942. Visit the old passages which run underneath the main streets, the maritime museum and the area known as the Quay.

THE TEA:
Tea is served in the elegant dining room overlooking the Cathedral. After a day spent sightseeing tuck into a traditional afternoon or, still the most popular, a cream tea. Price: from £4.

OPEN:
Daily from 3.30pm to around 5.30.

GETTING THERE:
Exeter is on the A30, A377 roads. Nearest motorway M5. Restricted parking in the town centre.

Silk and velvet put out the kitchen fire.

Thatched Cottage

Sprytown, Lifton
Telephone: (01566) 784224

Just a hundred yards from the A30, well known for its Devon cream teas, is apleasing thatched cottage is set in two-and-a-half acres of garden. It offers visitors a relaxed and friendly welcome and tea can be taken in the lounge, restaurant or garden.

What to see:

Nearby Launceston is an old fashioned market town, with a beautifully carved church, well worth visiting. From here you can visit the romantic and inspiring north Cornish coast, or head inland to wild Bodmin Moor to discover hidden unspoilt villages. The whole area is steeped in mystery and full of Arthurian legends.

THE TEA:
Guests can enjoy a range of tempting sandwiches, light scones and some good home baked cakes served by welcoming staff. A selection of teas includes Indian, China, fruit and herbal. Price: from £3.

OPEN:
Daily, throughout the year, from 8.30am to 9.30pm. Including Christmas and New Year.

GETTING THERE:
Lifton is situated on the A30 between Okehampton and Launceston. Nearest motorway M5. Parking is possible.

If you are cold tea will warm you – if you are heated it will cool you . . . – WE Gladstone

THE TEA:

The things that come out best are the simplest – at breakfast, lunch or tea. Cucumber sandwiches, freshly baked scones and a variety of cake and pastry treats served with generous helpings of tea account for the old English tea. Price: from £4.

OPEN:

Monday to Saturday from 10.30am to around 6.00pm. Sunday from 2-6.00pm.

GETTING THERE:

Chagford is on the A382. Nearest motorway M5 Parking is possible in the town.

There are none so blind as those who will not see.

THE TEA:

If you're really hungry try favourites such as omelettes or rarebits. Other treats are the afternoon teas with cakes, scones and teacakes. There are good choices of tea, so try something different. Price: from £3.

OPEN:

Monday to Saturday from 9.00am to 5.00pm. Closed on Sundays and Christmas and New Year.

GETTING THERE:

Blandford Forum is on the A354 A350 A357 roads. Nearest motorways M3 M5. Parking in the town.

Honest heart never lied.

Whiddons

High Street, Chagford
Telephone: (01647) 433406

Just a few steps from the church, this particular place draws a loyal following, especially for tea and cake. Passers-by who stop to browse amongst the book collections usually end up staying for the well rounded food as well. Fellow visitors, to this corner of Devon, may well include a famous face or two.

What to see:

The church of Saint Michael, built during prosperous tin mining times, has an interesting story threaded around it. On 11 October 1641 at the wedding of a Mary Whiddon, a jealous rival rushed up to the altar and shot and killed her. The story is later fictionalised in the novel *Lorna Doone* written by R.D. Blackmore.

Dorset

The Georgian Tea Room

Georgian Passage, Blandford Forum
Telephone: (01258) 450307

The first thing you'll notice walking into The Georgian Tea Room, is how small it is, just six or seven tables, and the second – how friendly the welcome is. Regulars and visitors are greeted in the same warm, generous fashion. The food here is simple and satisfying.

What to see:

The Bastard brothers, two local architects, rebuilt the town after fire destroyed most of it in 1731. It is Dorset's finest Georgian town. There are plenty of good drives around here, such as to Tollard Royal on a road full of hairpin bends but with superb views, when, and if, you arrive at the top.

The Horse with the Red Umbrella

High West Street, Dorchester
Telephone: (01305) 262019

Who thought up the delightful name? Nobody really seems to know! It describes itself as 'just a friendly place to eat.' That it certainly is. This tea room is just a warm, unpretentious place hung with any number of baskets, mugs and assorted what-nots.

What to see:

Even today Dorset must still look much as it must have looked two or three hundred years ago, or as Thomas Hardy describes it so incomparably well in his novels. If pilgrimages appeal to you, Hardy's birthplace, his home and old Stinsford Church where his heart is buried, all lie within a small radius of Dorchester.

THE TEA:

The window jam-packed with fresh bread, biscuits, cakes and pastries will beckon you inside. In addition there are light lunches and snacks Price: from £3.

OPEN:

Monday to Saturday from 8.00am to 5.00pm Closed Sunday and Bank Holidays.

GETTING THERE:

Dorchester is on the A37, A354 A352 roads Limited parking in the town.

Care and diligence bring luck.

King Alfred's Kitchen

Shaftesbury
Telephone: (01747) 852147

This is a dream for lovers of old houses and nirvana for low beamed ceiling buffs. You'll discover King Alfred's tucked away in a corner of the square at the top of Gold Hill. Not much has changed since 1400 or so. Amble through the door, admiring the timbers and fireplaces on your way to an old settle and table.

What to see:

King Canute died at Shaftesbury, and the remains of King Edward (murdered at Corfe Castle), were brought here. This ancient town is perched high on a hilltop overlooking the Blackmore Vale, and from its centre the picturesque cobbled street of Gold Hill makes a steep descent. Visit the Church and museum. All around are other places of historic or scenic interest.

THE TEA:

The kitchen delivers a small but outstanding selection of snacks, lunches and afternoon teas. The cakes are moist and the scones are served with can-I-lick-my-spoon clotted cream. The teas aren't bad either. Price: from £3.50.

OPEN:

Monday to Saturday from 9.30am to 5.30pm. Closed Sundays. Winter, open later from 11.00am.

GETTING THERE:

Shaftesbury is on the A30 A350 roads. Nearest motorways M3 M5 Limited parking in the town.

A baker's wife may bite of a bun.

47

Marigold Cottage

High Street, Spetisbury
Telephone: (01258) 452468

Friendly, easy-going and informal, this delightful beamed tea room in a thatched cottage has become a favourite with local families as well as visitors to the area. Tea in the garden surrounded by honeysuckle and climbing roses, is particularly enjoyable.

What to see:
The town of Blandford Forum was almost completely destroyed by fire in 1731 and was rebuilt in the Georgian style, with a very grand church. From here there are enjoyable drives to the Dorset coast, as well as many places of historical interest. Blandford was Thomas Hardy's 'Shottesford Forum'.

THE TEA:
As well as a Dorset cream tea there's always a selection of sandwiches, savouries, and delicious home-baked cakes served with fine choices of tea. Price: from £2.50.

OPEN:
Tuesday to Sunday 7.00am to 5.30pm. Closed Monday.

GETTING THERE:
Spetisbury is on the A350 (Blandford Forum) road. Own car park.

If fortune torments me, hope contents me.

Mortons House Hotel

Corfe Castle
Telephone: (01929) 480988

Mortons is one of Dorset's undiscovered jewels standing under the watchful eye of Corfe Castle, to which it is linked by underground tunnels. Enjoy a refreshing stop for an afternoon, a night or a week. Those who have tasted the style, flavour and character of the hotel once, invariably return.

What to see:
A visit to Corfe can be magical. The castle is magnificent and the area offers miles of unspoilt, idyllic scenery. There are bird and wildlife sanctuaries, golf courses and numerous opportunities for sport. The Purbeck coastline is designated as an 'area of outstanding natural beauty' with dramatic cliff walks, sandy beaches and solitary bays and coves.

THE TEA:
During the season afternoon teas, featuring scones and pastries, are served in the lounge or, in the walled gardens overlooking the thatched roofs of the village. Price: from £4.

OPEN:
During the summer months tea is served from 3-6.00pm. In winter, weekends only. Please check. Large parties can pre-book.

GETTING THERE:
Corfe Castle is on the A351. Nearest motorways M3 M27. Parking in the village.

Kissing goes by favour.

Potter In

19 Durngate Street, Dorchester
Telephone: (01305) 260312

In the often busy market town of Dorchester, an excellent choice to stop for tea is the Potter In. The food here is simple and good, service is friendly and if the weather's good take tea in the pretty garden.

What to see:
Dorchester is the 'Casterbridge' of Thomas Hardy's novels. Max Gate, which Hardy built and where he spent the last years of his life, lies on the town's outskirts. The cottage where he was born is at Higher Bockhampton. The lodgings of the infamous Judge Jeffreys, and the Old Crown Court, where the Tolpuddle Martyrs were sentenced are all of interest. The court room is open to the public.

THE TEA:
Throughout the day there are wholefood scones and cakes to have with a good cup of tea. There are at least twelve choices of tea, and 27 choices of ice-cream. Price: from £2.50.

OPEN:
Monday to Saturday 10.00am to 5.00pm. July and August open Sunday. Closed Sunday in Winter. Open Bank Holidays.

GETTING THERE:
Dorchester is on the A35, A37 and A354 roads. Town car parks.

Keep something for a rainy day.

Slepe Cottage Tea Rooms

Lytchett Minster, Dorchester Road
Telephone: (01929) 459281

Visitors come from far and wide to this pretty, thatched cottage that's well known for its cream teas. Get there early to get a table inside the cosy tea room, or better still, in the lovely old garden.

What to see:
All around the area there are interesting places to visit. Wareham is a fascinating old town, Poole Harbour, one of the loveliest natural harbours in the world, Corfe Castle, Lulworth Cove and Bere Regis (with Thomas Hardy associations), to name but a few.

THE TEA:
Set teas are available, including the famous cream tea, with super scones and clotted cream. Alternatively you can choose sandwiches and delicious home-made cakes served with a choice of teas. Price: from £3.50.

OPEN:
Monday to Sunday 10.30am to 5.30pm throughout the year, except Christmas and all of January.

GETTING THERE:
Lytchett Minster is on the A35 Poole-Dorchester road. Own car park.

Eat your brown bread first, it is a good thing to do.

Blake House Craft Centre

Blake End, Rayne
Telephone: (013763) 20662

When in the area, do make a little detour to this craft centre housed in a group of converted period farm buildings. There's a host of other small businesses to browse around, including rocks and fossils, fashion and antique shops. Tea is served in a tiny corner of the craft shop – crammed with hand-made gifts, pottery, dried flowers and small watercolours. On sunny afternoons, tables and chairs are moved out onto the grass for picnic teas where peacocks roam at random.

What to see:
This is the main route to the picturesque village of Finchingfield.

THE TEA:
Plump, fruit or wholemeal scones and slices of home-made cake go well with steaming pots of tea. Price: from £2.

OPEN:
Tuesday to Sunday 10.30am to 6.00pm. Closed Monday except Bank Holidays.

GETTING THERE:
The craft centre is located off the A120 at Saling Oak, between Braintree and Dunmow. Nearest motorway M11. Own car park.

Such beginning, such end.

The Causeway Tea Cottage

Finchingfield
Telephone: (01371) 810431

Winding lanes through the Essex countryside bring you to the attractive village of Finchingfield. The Causeway Tea Cottage, situated on the embankment facing the village pond, bustles with families and friends enjoying themselves. It's warm and cosy inside the oak-beamed tea room, with its large inglenook, tiny windows and tables already laid for tea.

What to see:
Coming in from the west, the visitor to the village will see its pond and bridge, and the houses which line the road climbing the hill towards the Church of St John the Baptist – a perfect village scene! Patrick Brontë, father of Charlotte and Emily, was curate of Finchingfield between 1806 and 1808.

THE TEA:
A set tea of brown and white buttered bread, scones with preserve and cream and a selection of traditional cakes and biscuits – served with pots of Indian, Earl Grey or herb teas. Price: £3.

OPEN:
Daily 10.30am to 5.30pm. Closed Thursday morning and for two months – December and January.

GETTING THERE:
Finchingfield is to the north-west of Braintree on the B1053. Limited parking in the village.

Better to ask the way then go astray.

The Cake Table

Fishmarket Street, Thaxted
Telephone: (01371) 831206

Tucked away on a street close to the magnificent Guild Hall, built in 1390 when the town prospered because of its cutlery industry, is the delightfully unassuming Cake Table. In the simply furnished tea room there is an open brick fireplace and a dresser full of scones, pastries and cakes that even the strongest amongst you will find irresistible! Here, amid shared tables, friendly chatter and attentive service, afternoons pass most agreeably.

What to see:
Dominated by its hilltop medieval church and the magnificent Guildhall, a walk around Thaxted is full of interest.

THE TEA:
The choice is not a simple one. Shall it be a buttery scone, a slice of home-made bread, or a piece of the English fruit cake? There is an interesting choice of loose leaf teas as well as herb and fruit infusions. Price: from £2.50.

OPEN:
Tuesday to Sunday 11.00am to 5.00pm throughout the year.

GETTING THERE:
Thaxted is well signposted on the B1051 or B184. Ample parking in the town.

Fair face fair heart.

The Crooked Cottage Tea Rooms

The Quay, Burnham-on-Crouch
Telephone: (01621) 783868

The view across the quay is splendid from this three-hundred year old cottage tea room. The service is relaxed and friendly and in the summer months the old rose garden is a delightful setting for tea.

What to see:
Like other estuary towns in Essex, Burnham-on-Crouch is noted as a centre for yachting and oyster breeding. The small museum has local maritime and agricultural exhibits. Nearby Southend-on-Sea still retains a unique place as the closest seaside resort to London, with entertainment for all the family.

THE TEA:
There is a good range of freshly made sandwiches, home-made cakes and cream teas. Darjeeling, Earl Grey and Lapsang Souchong are just some of the sixteen teas offered. Price: from £3.

OPEN:
Tuesday to Sunday 10.00am to 6.00pm. Closed Monday except Bank Holidays.

GETTING THERE:
Burnham-on-Crouch is on the B1010 and B1021 roads. Nearest motorway M25. Car parking in the town.

When fortune smiles upon thee take the advantage of it.

*made in a large Cafetière pot

Dear Patricia
        Thankyou for your letter
I am really a coffee person
but if ever I drink tea I enjoy
a pot of Earl Grey (loose leaves), or
mint-tea made with fresh mint*.
        Best wishes with your book
                                Una Stubbs

NIGEL HAWTHORNE

Dear Patricia Rose Cress —
        Thank you for your letter
inviting me to comment on tea.
Forgive if I don't respond other
than to say that now and again
I enjoy drinking it

                Nigel Hawthorne

The Essex Rose Tea House

High Street, Dedham
Telephone: (01206) 323101

The unspoilt black and white exterior of this house has instant appeal, while the interior is traditional and welcoming. Tables are set close together on the wooden floors, pictures and paintings cover the walls. It's a lively, bustling spot, the meeting place for local people as well as visitors. Here you'll discover a wealth of gift items you didn't know you needed!

What to see:
Picturesque Dedham is, of course celebrated for its Constable connection, and has many interesting and historic buildings. The valley of the River Stour is one of the most beautiful in England, still much as it was when Constable painted landscapes here, and well provided with footpaths.

Philpott's Tea Rooms

Lychgate House, Church St. Waltham Abbey
Telephone: (01992)767641

Without wishing to be unkind to Waltham Abbey, to find a tea room of this quality was a very pleasant surprise. Not far from the town centre, this small 15th-century house looks out over the Abbey and Churchyard. The interior is more or less as it has been for the last four hundred years – oak cross beams, small windows and an inglenook fireplace. Sitting at one of the small tables, enjoying tea, you may have the feeling you could easily turn back the clock!

What to see:
As well as the Abbey Church, there is a local museum in Sun Street. The five thousand acres of Epping Forest are close by.

THE TEA:
The fixed price tea menu is good value. A cream tea of two scones, butter, fresh cream and strawberry jam costs from £3.60p. A range of teas includes Ceylon, Earl Grey, Darjeeling and house blend.

OPEN:
Daily 9.00am to 6.00pm Closed over the Christmas holiday.

GETTING THERE:
Dedham is on the B1029. Designated parking in the village.

Nature will have its course.

THE TEA:
Philpott's offers scones, bread and butter, cakes and pastries. The set tea is available from 2.00pm onwards. Price: from £4.

OPEN:
Daily from 9.00am to some time after 4.00pm (except Christmas Day!).

GETTING THERE:
Waltham Abbey is to the north-east of London and can be approached via the M25, A121. Parking is possible in the side streets of the town.

Water is the king of food.

53

Two Tees

High Street, Bures
Telephone: (01787) 228335

Two Tees is so unpretentious from the outside that you may be tempted to go no further than the front door. But give it a chance. Inside you'll find an old cottage front room with four or five tables covered with gingham cloths and, more importantly, a bit of peace and quiet. It's a place where people pop in to enjoy a home-made cake, and a strong, hot cuppa!

What to see:

Bures is well placed for exploring the surrounding countryside. Nearby are 'Roman' Colchester and Constable's East Bergholt, the old villages of Suffolk many with great churches and much more besides; the list is endless. And everywhere rolling English countryside and shaded cottage gardens.

THE TEA:

The menu is simple: home-made cakes and scones served on an appealing assortment of china. There's a good selection of Indian, China, herbal and fruit teas. Price: cream teas from £2.

OPEN:

Daily from 10.00am to 5.00pm. Closed over Christmas.

GETTING THERE:

Bures is on the B1508 Colchester to Sudbury road. Parking in the village.

A full cup must be carried steadily.

Gloucestershire

Ann's Pantry

Market Place, Cirencester
Telephone: (01285) 653505

Ann's Pantry is a busy, bustling tea room, two in fact, above a baker's shop. The cake table is the afternoon centrepiece with a selection of chocolate, cream and fruit gateaux.

What to see:

In Roman Britain, Cirencester was the second most important town, and the Corinium Museum has many Roman artefacts. In the 15th century the town prospered with the growth of the wool trade, and the church of St John the Baptist is known as one of the greatest wool churches in the county. There are many well-preserved old buildings in the town.

THE TEA:

A selection of cream teas is also served from 2.00pm onwards. Tea choices include Darjeeling, Earl Grey and Lapsang Souchong. Price: from £3.50.

OPEN:

Monday to Saturday 9.00am to 5.00pm. Sunday 3.00 to 5.00pm.

GETTING THERE:

Cirencester is on the A419, A429 and A433 roads. Nearest motorways M4 and M5. Town car parks.

All clouds bring not rain.

Black Cat

High Street, Lechlade on Thames
Telephone: (01367) 252273

In Lechlade's busy high street, is this extended, snug tea room. The interior is simplicity itself with wooden chairs, coloured tablecloths, plain white walls and a few prints. Here you'll find home-cooking served by helpful ladies – you'll be well looked after.

What to see:

Lechlade has a wide main street with attractive houses and shops. The tall church spire can be seen for miles around. Within easy reach is the Vale of the White Horse, the old Ridgeway Path runs here, with Wayland's Smithy close by, and the white horse itself cut out of the turf on the chalk downs.

THE TEA:
A selection of sandwiches and cakes complements a cream tea of scones, cream and strawberry jam. A range of teas include Orange Pekoe, Earl Grey and Lapsang Souchong. Price: from £3.

OPEN:
Monday to Saturday 9.30am to 6.00pm. Sunday 12 noon to 6.00pm.

GETTING THERE:
Lechlade is north-west of Faringdon on the A417. Free, limited parking in the centre of the village.

A kind heart loseth nought at last.

Jenny Wren

The Street, Bibury
Telephone: (01285740) 555

From the beamed cottage tea room – with a Cotswold stone fireplace – climb the ancient steps to the pretty rooftop garden and enjoy an unhurried country afternoon tea.

What to see:

Described as 'the most beautiful village' in the Cotswolds, Bibury attracts a lot of visitors. Many of the honey coloured cottages look onto the little River Coln, complete with wooden bridge. The main attractions of the village are the Saxon church, the Arlington Mill Museum – housed in a 17th-century corn mill – and the local trout farm.

Give me tea sweet and weak
Bring me The Times and do not speak.
– A.P. Herbert

THE TEA:
There are choices of home-made cakes, biscuits and cream gateaux in addition to the clotted cream tea. There is a selection of Indian, China and fruit tea blends. Price: set tea from £3.30.

OPEN:
Monday to Sunday 10.00am to 5.30pm throughout the year. Closed Christmas.

GETTING THERE:
Bibury is on the B4425. Nearest motorway M4. Parking in the village..

THE TEA:

Afternoon tea brings a feast of fresh scones with preserves and clotted cream plus lots of delicious cakes and pastries. A choice of tea blends is offered. Price: from £3.

OPEN:

Monday to Sunday 9.00am to 9.00pm, throughout the year.

GETTING THERE:

Moreton-in-Marsh is on the A44. Public car park and street parking.

---◇---

Among friends all things are common.

---◇---

The Marshmallow

High Street, Moreton-in-Marsh
Telephone: (01608) 651536

Once in a while, if you are lucky, you may come across a particular kind of tea shop. It fits no particular pattern and obeys no edict of fashion. And yet you know from the moment you walk through the door that you have found a perfect spot. The Marshmallow is one such place.

What to see:

The wide main street of Moreton-in-Marsh is actually built on the Roman Fosse Way. The street contains handsome historic houses and a curfew tower with its bell still in place. All around are gently rounded hills and wooded valleys with quiet villages, old churches and richly endowed manor houses.

---◇---

THE TEA:

A comprehensive menu is served, but set afternoon teas, eight in all, are a speciality here. Next comes a satisfying range of home-made scones, cakes and pies. Good choices of tea end the afternoon. Price: from £3.

OPEN:

Tuesday to Saturday from 10.00am to 5.00pm. Sunday from 11.00am to 5.00pm. Closed Monday except Bank Holidays.

GETTING THERE:

Winchcombe is NE of Cheltenham on the B4632. Nearest motorway M5. Limited parking in the town.

The Olde Bakery

High Street, Winchcombe
Telephone: (01242) 602469

The very name conjures up the setting, and for many regulars and visitors alike this is a popular stop for tea, the atmosphere lending itself to chatting amicably with the table next door. All of which is very comforting: no chaps with Mohican haircuts or girls in cowboy boots.

What to see:

Two stone coffins in the church at Winchcombe are believed to be those of Kenulf of Mercia and his son and therefore over a thousand years old. Catherine of Aragon is believed to have stitched one of the altar cloths. South of Winchcombe is Belas Knap an unusual Stone Age burial mound with a false portal and burial chambers opening in the sides.

---◇---

Fill what you will, drink what you will.

---◇---

Old Lady Tea Shop

1 Threadneedle Street, Stroud
Telephone: (01453) 762441

Just a few steps from the High Street, this popular bakery and cake shop also serves tea. Climb the stairs and you'll discover a quaint, parlour-style tea room that's cool in the summer, cosy in the winter, and always welcoming.

What to see:

Surrounded by glorious hill country, Stroud was once one of the most important centres for the manufacture of broadcloth. Its history is traced in the local museum, one of the most interesting in the county. It illustrates old methods of cloth weaving and old crafts.

Small Talk Tea Room

High Street, Bourton-on-the-Water
Telephone: (014518) 21596

Outside is the picturesque village square – inside are bow windows, low beams, lace tablecloths, pretty china and an appetising array of home-baked cakes and pastries. On fine days tea can be taken outside.

What to see:

The River Windrush flows through the village under low stone bridges – it is a picturesque spot and is popular with visitors. Two more pretty villages are Upper and Lower Slaughter. Their name derives from the Anglo-Saxon word 'slough' meaning muddy place. All are best visited out of high season.

THE TEA:
A simple menu offers sandwiches, scones, teacakes and a selection of cream and fruit cakes, served with a small choice of teas. Price: from £2.50.

OPEN:
Tuesday to Saturday 9.30am to 4.30pm. Monday and Thursday until 4.00pm. Closed Sunday and bank holidays.

GETTING THERE:
Stroud is on the A46 and A419 roads. Nearest motorway M5. Public car parks.

---

*No bees, no honey;
no work, no money.*

THE TEA:
Set teas feature home-made scones, cream and tasty preserves. Moist, light cakes are very tempting as are the fruit pies. There's a good choice of teas including Indian, China and herbal. Price: set tea from £3.

OPEN:
Monday to Sunday 9.00am to 5.30pm. Closed over Christmas and New Year.

GETTING THERE:
Bourton-on-the-Water is on the A429. Car park and street parking.

'Tis never too late for delight.

Tea at the Peggums

Church Street, Stow-on-the-Wold
Telephone: (014518) 30102

Generous portions are as much a feature of Peggums, as is the charming welcome from the owners. Step down into the old beamed cottage and enjoy the convivial atmosphere and good home baking.

What to see:

This is the highest town in the Cotswolds, and was once the thriving centre of the wool industry. Fine old houses cluster around the Market Square, and just off it, is the church of St Edward where Cromwell kept a thousand Royalist prisoners after one of his victories. Each age, from Norman times down to the present, has added something of interest to the church.

Wintor House

Church Street, Tewkesbury
Telephone: (01684) 292703

A couple of minutes walk along the main street of this fascinating town leads to this very traditional tea room. The house dates back to the 15th century and has aged with charm and grace through the five-hundred or so years since it was built.

What to see:

This is an old town, site of a Yorkist victory in the Wars of the Roses. The abbey is magnificent with a 132 foot Norman tower, and what is fascinating is the number of alleyways which lead from the main streets of the town, about thirty in all. It is a most delightful town to explore on foot.

Retire to tea and scandal according to their ancient custom.
– William Congreve

THE TEA:
Only the finest ingredients are used in making flavoursome teabreads, light scones and home-made cakes. Care has been taken to provide a fine choice of excellent teas. Price: from £2.50.

OPEN:
Saturday and Sunday only, 3.00 to 6.00pm.

GETTING THERE:
Stow-on-the-Wold is on the A424, A429 and A436 roads. Nearest motorway M40. Parking in the Square.

There is a great deal of poetry and fine sentiment in a chest of tea.
– RW Emerson

THE TEA:
Set afternoon teas are served with light scones and a choice of home-made cakes, accompanied by Earl Grey, China or tea from India. Prices: from £3.

OPEN:
Tuesday to Saturday 10.00am to 5.30pm, Sunday 12.00 to 5.30pm. Winter 10.00am to 2.30pm. Closed Monday.

GETTING THERE:
Tewkesbury is on the A38 and A438 roads. Nearest motorways M5 and M50. Town centre car parks.

Bush House Tea Rooms

Selborne
Telephone: (01420) 511339

Selborne is a traditional country village with a touch of history, and Bush House plays a proper part: centuries old family house, with inglenook fireplaces, old polished tables and chairs, and a charming, flower filled garden. The baking here is unfussy, homely and familiar.

What to see:

The village is most attractive with houses that have changed little over the centuries, while the church dates from 1180. In the churchyard grows a yew tree which is reputed to be seven hundred years old. Selborne has long been associated with the naturalist Reverend Gilbert White (1720-1793). The Wakes which was his home is now a museum containing many items of interest.

THE TEA:
A choice of two set teas can include warm scones, freshly made sandwiches and a selection of fine teas with such delights as cherry and coconut, fruit slices and walnut and chocolate cakes. Price: from £3.

OPEN:
Monday to Sunday 11.00am to 5.30pm. Closed Tuesday Christmas and all of January.

GETTING THERE:
Selborne is off the A31 on the B3006. Nearest motorway M3. Village car park.

Better be happy than wise.

Cassandra's Cup

Chawton, near Alton
Telephone: (01420) 83144

Across the road from Jane Austen's house, in an idyllic village setting you will discover a small, pretty and friendly tea room. After tea there are two rooms to browse in for small gifts and old china items.

What to see:

Jane Austen lived in a simple red brick house in Chawton from 1809-1817. She wrote 'Emma', 'Persuasion' and 'Mansfield park' while here. Her house contains a museum with various of her personal effects and is open to the public. Please check opening times. She is buried in Winchester Cathedral.

The Golden age was never the present age.

THE TEA:
From 2.30pm afternoon teas are served, with a good range of excellent home-baking. There are wholesome scones, several cakes and a moist fruit loaf. Tea blends include Earl Grey, Darjeeling and rosehip. Price: set tea from £2.75.

OPEN:
Daily 10.30am to 5.00pm. Closed Mondays and Tuesdays from November to April and weekdays in February.

GETTING THERE:
Chawton is one mile south of Alton on the A32 road. Nearest motorway M3. Parking in the village.

THE TEA:

Look out for plump scones, buttery shortbread, iced chocolate sponges and tangy lemon cheesecake, all of which go beautifully with an excellent pot of Indian or herbal tea. Price: set tea from £3.

OPEN:

Tuesday to Saturday 10.00am to 5.30pm. Closed Sunday and Monday, two weeks September/October and one week Christmas and New Year.

GETTING THERE:

Romsey is on the A31 and A3057 roads. Nearest motorways M3 and M27. Car parking in the town.

Cherry year, a merry year a plum year a glum year.

THE TEA:

The afternoon set tea menu lists a cream tea as well as four or five house specials. Home-made cakes include chocolate, fruit, coffee, Victoria and date and walnut. Price: from £2.95.

OPEN:

Daily 10.00am to 6.00pm. From 2.00pm for tea.

GETTING THERE:

Burley is south-west of Southampton off the A31. Own car park.

Cobweb Tea Rooms

49 The Hundred, Romsey
Telephone: (01794) 516434

It is worth making a trip to Romsey for afternoon tea at this cosy, beamed tea room with a charming walled garden. The tea table is laden with all sorts of goodies, and the atmosphere is most welcoming.

What to see:

The town of Romsey is famous for its abbey church. Except for the west front, the abbey is mainly 12th century. There are some interesting treasures to be seen including the deed of sale signed by Henry VIII. A statue of Lord Palmerston stands in the market square and his former home Broadlands is open to the public. It is now popular with visitors because of its connection with Lord Mountbatten.

Forest Tea House

Pound Lane, Burley
Telephone: (0142540) 2305

The Forest House tea rooms are part of a country cottage only a few hundred yards away from the centre of Burley Village. On sunny days you can enjoy tea in the well-kept country garden. There is a tranquil and informal atmosphere.

What to see:

Burley is an attractive village and makes a good centre for exploring this part of the New Forest. Castle Hill, an ancient earthwork, gives good views of the area. Beaulieu, Salisbury, Winchester and Bournemouth are but a short drive away.

Truth has a good face.

Manor Farm Tea Rooms

Ringwood Road, Burley
Telephone: (01425) 402218

Manor Farm, from the outside, captures the atmosphere of an old-fashioned, thatched, country tea room of 40 or 50 years ago. Push open the front door, and discover a place of beams, log fires, nooks and corners. It's all rather seductive and captivating and proves you can have your cake and eat it!

What to see:
Visitors to this area are within easy reach of Romsey, Salisbury, Winchester and Bournemouth. From Southampton there are trips to the Isle of Wight. London is less than 2 hours away. The auburn and gold colours of the New Forest are superb during the autumn months of September and October.

THE TEA:
If the heart of the place is reassuringly old fashioned, the set teas offer something for all tastes. In the afternoon there are 8 or 9 variations to choose from. Price: from £2.50 to £5.50.

OPEN:
Tuesday to Saturday 10.00am-5.00pm. Sunday 10.30-5.00pm. Closed Christmas, Boxing Day and 2 weeks in January.

GETTING THERE:
On the Ringwood Road, nearest routes, A338, A31 and the M3. Own car park.

A kind heart loseth nought at last.

Splashes Tea Shoppe

High Street, Brockenhurst
Telephone: (01590) 622120

Take a walk through the village of Brockenhurst and you'll come across this shop selling cards, prints and small gift items. A cream tea can be enjoyed in the tiny tea room that adjoins the shop or, spread out on the patio for scones, sunning and gossip.

What to see:
On the southern edge of the New Forest, this attractive village with thatched cottages has a ford in its main street. The church is mainly Norman and a yew tree in the church yard is reputed to be 1000 years old. The village is ideally placed for visiting the New Forest, with its many trails and picnic areas.

THE TEA:
There are slices of home-made cakes, or a choice of set teas such as the 'Hovis'. A snip of teas includes Indian, Earl Grey, China and lemon. Price: from £2.50.

OPEN:
Monday to Saturday 9.15am to 5.30pm. Closed Sunday.

GETTING THERE:
Brockenhurst is on the A337 south of Lyndhurst. Parking in the village.

Content lodges oftener in cottages than palaces.

Dear Patricia Rose Cross,

I am writing to say how much I have enjoyed eating and shopping at the Copshaw Kitchen, Newcastleton, over the past 13 years. It is a treasure-trove of glass, china, & antique textiles & I have gained much inspiration for my rug designs — see enclosed — from my visits there. Guests from further afield are always amazed by the high quality of the Scotch baking & by the amazing value for money. It — & Jean Elliot — deserve a good write-up in your book.

Yours sincerely,
Emma Tennant.

The Village Tea Rooms

High Street, Hamble
Telephone: (01703) 455583

Tucked away in the river-side village of Hamble is this old characterful building dating from the 17th century. It was at one time a rope-makers/coffin-makers business but has been transformed into a welcoming, cosy tea room, offering home baking Hampshire style.

What to see:

Once a quiet fishing village Hamble is now a popular boating and yachting centre with an annual regatta in July. The old part of the village and the wharf are still very attractive and there is plenty to do and see. From the common there are views over the New Forest and Southampton Water.

Hereford & Worcester
The Elms

Abberley
Telephone: (01299) 896666

The Elms is a country house hotel, near Abberley in Hereford & Worcester, that actually feels like a home from home. That is, if your home is a lovely Queen Anne house set in ten acres of well kept gardens and lawns.

What to see:

Two churches are of interest in the village of Abberley. An attractive country church which is partly in ruins and a rather grand Victorian church, which lies just outside the village. The church at Great Witley is also worth visiting for the richness of its baroque interior. Abberley has an unchanging charm

---

*Tea, although an Oriental
Is a gentleman's drink at least. – Anon*

THE TEA:

Nice scones and shortbread, and tempting cakes go well with a refreshing pot of tea. There's a pretty garden for outdoor tea in fine weather. Price: from £2.65.

OPEN:

Monday to Friday 9.00am to 5.00pm (4.30pm winter). Weekends 9.30am to 6.00pm.

GETTING THERE:

Hamble is signposted off the A27. Nearest motorways M3 and M27. Village car park.

Hunger breaks through stone walls.

THE TEA:

The lounges of this imposing mansion make an elegant setting for afternoon tea. Biscuits, scones and cakes are all made on the premises, and locally grown strawberries and cream are available in season. There is a selection of very good teas as well as refreshing infusions such as peppermint. Price: set tea from £6.

OPEN:

Daily 3.00 to 6.00pm.

GETTING THERE:

Abberley is on the A443 and A451 roads. Nearest motorway M5. Ample car parking.

THE TEA:

Servings are always generous of the tasty scones and lovely cream cakes. A choice of teas includes Darjeeling and Earl Grey. Price: from £2.

OPEN:

Monday to Saturday 9.00am to 5.00pm. Closed Sunday.

GETTING THERE:

Pershore is on the A44 and A4104 roads. Nearest motorway M5. Town car parks.

We live in stirring times,
tea stirring times.
Christopher Isherwood

Sugar 'n' Spice

20 High Street, Pershore
Telephone: (01386) 553654

The entrance to this welcoming, informal tea room is through a glassware and china shop. The tables always look inviting with lace cloths and Wedgwood china and the menu provides plenty of variety. Service is kind and thoughtful.

What to see:

Pershore is a particularly charming historic town on the River Avon. It is situated in the heart of a fruit growing area, notably plums. The beautiful ruins of the Benedictine Abbey church were preserved because the local population paid to keep it for their own worship. A medieval stone bridge of six arches crosses the Avon.

THE TEA:

Look out for the Dutch apple flan and the baked cheesecake, as well as a good range of sandwiches, gateaux and fruit tarts. 'Tea of the week' may offer a flinty Keemun or a delicately perfumed jasmine. Price: from £3.

OPEN:

Monday to Wednesday and Saturday 10.30am to 5.00pm, Sunday 11.00am to 5.00pm. Closed Thursday.

GETTING THERE:

Broadway is on the A44, six miles south-east of Evesham. Parking in the village.

Tisanes

The Green, Broadway
Telephone: (01386) 852112

An elegant shop that specialises in both useful and frivolous tea accessories for home and table, including a wide variety of teapots, china and a range of teas too numerous to list.

What to see:

Broadway is a village of old cottages and fine gabled houses, it is one of the beauty spots of the Cotswolds and popular with tourists. At different times both Charles I and Oliver Cromwell stayed at the old manor house, now a hotel. South of the village is Broadway Tower Country Park.

Tea thou soft, thou sober,
Sage, and venerable liquid.
Colley Cibber

Battlers Green Farm

Common Lane, Radlett
Telephone: (01923) 857505

If you have been promising yourself for ages that you will visit a local farm, now is the time to discover one, especially, if it is as good as Battlers Green Farm. Still a working farm it comes complete with craft shop, pet supplies and tea room. Take a seat in the timbered barn where the aromas of home baking waft through the door.

What to see:
Hertfordshire appears to be one of those counties that visitors drive through on their way to more renowned areas of England, but it has much to offer in the way of quiet country villages and uncrowded roads. Ayot St Lawrence, the last home of George Bernard Shaw, Hatfield Palace and Knebworth are three of the most famous attractions.

THE TEA:
There's a selection of generous tea time treats such as rarebits, scrambled eggs, and tea breads as well as 3 set teas. The accompanying leaf list is well chosen and includes Indian, China and fruit. Price: from £3.50.

OPEN:
Monday to Friday from 9.30am to 4.30pm. Weekends until 5.30pm.

GETTING THERE:
The A5183 runs through Radlett. Nearest motorway M25. Parking at the farm.

As they brew so let them drink.

The Castle Tea Rooms

14 Castle Street, Berkhamsted
Telephone: (01442) 866974

Enter into the Castle Tea Rooms and step back to the age of the Edwardian parlour. Comfortable tables and chairs, period fittings, alcoves and corners filled with plates, pictures, newspapers and books, all add to that special period atmosphere. A ritual at this comfortable tea room is to wander over to the dresser where all the cakes and pastries are displayed to see what's new and what looks appealing. The only problem is that as soon as you sit down, another cake or tart arrives from the kitchen looking just as delicious as the one you ordered!

What to see:
A walk around the town will bring you to the castle ruins.

THE TEA:
You may decide on a Fireside Tea – coddled egg (served in Victorian dishes), toast and scones with all the trimmings – from £3. Or perhaps a pot of tea and a slice or two of Bakewell tart.

OPEN:
Tuesday to Saturday 10.00am to 5.30pm, Sunday and Bank Holidays 12 noon to 5.30pm. Closed Monday.

GETTING THERE:
Berkhamsted is on the main A41. Parking in the town.

Better kiss a knave then be troubled by him.

Church Tea Rooms

Swan Street, Ashwell
Telephone: (01462) 742682 – for bookings

THE TEA:
Enjoy home-made cakes and scones served with strong cups of tea. All the proceeds go towards the church restoration fund.

OPEN:
Sunday only 2.30 to 5.00pm. Opening Sunday 4 March, closing the first Sunday in December.

GETTING THERE:
Ashwell is two miles north of the A505, Baldock to Royston road. Parking is possible in the village.

Truth is mighty and will prevail.

Ashwell is full of historic interest and appears to have been a prosperous village, except when interrupted by fire or the Black Death. The plague struck hard; this is clearly evoked by some of the writing on a wall inside the church tower. One says (in Latin): '1350. Miserable, wild, distracted, the dregs of the people alone survive'. After a walk around the village follow the 'teas' sign to discover home-made cakes and scones served in the old church rooms.

What to see:
Ashwell has some notable houses and inns! In Swan Street the small town hall is now a fascinating museum of local bygones.

The Old Swan Tea Shop

Hare Street Village, near Buntingford
Telephone: (01763) 289 265

THE TEA:
The menu is unpretentious and very reasonable in price. It features favourites like cream teas and assorted home-made cakes and biscuits, with a variety of teas.

OPEN:
April to October: Monday to Sunday 10.00am to 7.00pm. Closed Wednesdays. November to March: Thursday to Sunday 10.00am to 6.00pm. Closed Monday to Wednesday.

GETTING THERE:
Hare Street Village is north of Puckeridge on the B1368. Parking in the car park to the south side of the building.

Truth never grows old.

This is a place of beehives and birds, lilypond and swans, cobbles and flowers, and ivy clambering over old stone walls. It was originally a village inn, first granted a licence when Elizabeth 1 was on the throne, before that the inn-keepers were frequently imprisoned for serving ale without one! But times change and The Old Swan now specialises in serving home-cooked food and country fare.

What to see:
Great Hormead – a modest village of delightful cottages and Little Hormead with its tiny Norman church. A further drive will bring you to Hatfield, its most prized possession being the illustrious Hatfield House, built by Robert Cecil, between 1608 and 1612.

Rumballs Farm

Thorley
Telephone: (01279) 651441

Driving along the winding lanes, following all the notices that lead you to Rumballs Farm, you begin to feel as if you're really in the country; the only noise is the birds singing. The old barn has been tastefully and simply transformed into a charming craft centre, full of rustic crafts, beautiful embroidery and needlepoint patterns, as well as shelves of pretty fabrics.

In good weather, you can sip tea in the flower filled farmyard.

What to see:

The village of Much Hadham is full of interest. Edmund Tudor was born here, and distinguished residents have included William Morris and Henry Moore.

THE TEA:

The food is homely and traditional, including fruit and wholemeal scones, delicious shortbread, and slices of lemon cake, date and treacle and several more. Prices are very reasonable.

OPEN:

Tuesday to Saturday 10.30am to 5.00pm. Closed Sunday and Monday.

GETTING THERE:

Thorley is off the A1185 Bishop's Stortford to Sawbridgeworth road. Ample parking.

Friends tie their purse with a cobweb string.

Water Mill

Kingsbury, St Albans
Telephone: (017278) 53502

To include a Waffle House in a book about afternoon tea may be stretching things a bit far, but Kingsbury Mill is full of charm and waffles are a light type of pastry! The mill was identified on this site in the Domesday Book. The present mill dates back to the 16th century, and visitors can see the water-wheel churning and where the unmilled grain was delivered. The Waffle House forms part of the mill, and one steps into a room furnished with honey-coloured pine.

What to see:

Do visit the Tourist Information Centre in the Town Hall, Market Place.

THE TEA:

What is a waffle? A waffle is a light type of pastry cooked between two buttered and heated plates or a waffle iron. There is a choice of teas. Prices are reasonable.

OPEN:

Tuesday to Saturday 11.00am to 6.00pm (5.00pm winter), Sunday 12 noon to 6.00pm (5.00pm winter). Closed Monday.

GETTING THERE:

St Albans is well signposted off the M25, M10, M1 and A414; There are a number of central city car parks.

Soft fire makes sweet malt.

The Wishing Well

67 High Street, Kings Langley
Telephone: (01923) 260305

The Wishing Well brims with a haphazard sort of charm, warmly felt as you make your way past the front room, crammed with all sorts of colourful gift items, to the little back room for a pot of tea. The tea room with its white walls and red tablecloths has a welcoming atmosphere, and you'll find the exhibition of local artists work most interesting.

What to see:
The magnificent tomb of Edmund de Langley, brother of the Black Prince, is in the Church round the corner.

A good Jack makes a good Jill.

THE TEA:
This is the place to come for wholesome baking. Cakes may include apple cake, kiwi sponge, fruit buns and many more. Plain or wholemeal scones complement pots of Indian, Earl Grey or fruit teas. Prices are very reasonable.

OPEN:
Monday, Tuesday, Thursday, Friday 10.00am to 3.00pm, Saturday 10.00am to 5.00pm (tea all day).

GETTING THERE:
Kings Langley is on the main A41 Aylesbury Road. Parking is in the road (except rush hours) or in the free car park nearby.

Isle of Wight

The Batwing

Godshill
Telephone: (01983) 840 634

This modest, almost plain, cottage tea shop is in danger of being eclipsed by a burgeoning collection of assorted tea experiences! Visitors who do find it, however, are always grateful. In the low beamed rooms, traditionally furnished, are families and groups of friends reading, munching or quietly chatting.

What to see:
This is, probably the Isle of Wight's most photographed village – and not surprisingly, since the tower of the parish church rising from a cluster of cottages provides a picture-postcard combination of thatch and stone. You may find it over commercialised, but the older part of the village and the walk to the church are undeniably pretty. Visit in May and September.

THE TEA:
A limited range of light meals and snacks are offered as well as a selection of sandwiches, Home-made cakes and scones The ever popular clotted cream tea is priced at £2.50.

OPEN:
Daily during the season, March to end of October, 10.00am to 5.00pm. Closed in winter.

GETTING THERE:
Godshill is west of Shanklin on the A3020. Parking in the village.

They are welcome that bring.

Brighstone Tea Gardens

Brighstone
Telephone: (01983) 740229

The feeling of nostalgia is one reason why visitors enthuse about this place so much. The tea gardens were created in 1922 and have altered little since then. Relax on the veranda overlooking the rose gardens or inside one of the pavilion-style tea rooms and enjoy an atmosphere that hasn't been mucked about with.

What to see:

Nestling under a chalk ridge Brighstone is itself picturesque with an interesting history of smuggling. Coast and rolling countryside are equally lovely here. Small though the island is, the scenery is extraordinarily varied-and is at its best in spring and autumn, when visitors are few and the roads are empty.

THE TEA:

The menu offers a choice of light meals and snacks but the home-made clotted cream teas are still the all-time favourite. Well, you can't have enough of that, can you? Price from £3.

OPEN:

Daily from 10.00am to 5.00pm. Easter to the end of October only. Check if open in winter.

GETTING THERE:

Brighstone is signposted off the A3055, Ventnor to Yarmouth road. Parking in the village.

Time flies away without delay.

Gilly's Tea Rooms

High Street, Brading
Telephone: (01983) 407271

Brading has a lot to offer in the way of little attractions and when it comes to the food stakes, too, there is good reason to linger a while. Probably the best place for a spot of bib and tucker is Gilly's. It's not smart, it's not posh – but it has a 30's front parlour homely charm, and churns out plump honey-coloured 'just made' scones and cakes.

What to see:

For a very small town, Brading offers quite a lot: the town hall with stocks and whipping post, a Roman villa with mosaics, an interesting church, a waxworks and a small toy museum. Also close by is Nunwell House, visited by Charles I before his trial.

Say well or be still.

THE TEA:

The menu also offers tasty soups and snacks, salads and made-to-order sandwiches. There is always an enticing range of cakes and tray bakes all of which can be bought to eat at home with a pot of your favourite. Price: from £3.

OPEN:

Monday to Saturday 10.00am to 5.00pm. In winter Tuesday to Saturday 10.00am to 4.30pm. Closed all of January

GETTING THERE:

Brading is on the A3055 road. Parking is possible off the main narrow street.

THE TEA:

A range of straightforward snacks are available all day. Cakes, crumbles and tarts are on the tea menu, along with two set clotted cream teas. Price from £3.

OPEN:

Daily from 8.45am to 10.00pm. From 2.30 for tea. Closed end of October to March.

GETTING THERE:

Yarmouth is on the A3054 road. Parking is possible in and around the town.

Share and share alike.

THE TEA:

The afternoon wouldn't be complete without a clotted cream tea and a slice of cake. And speaking of cakes-there are usually five or six fresh from the oven. The most popular are chocolate and walnut. Price: from £3.50.

OPEN:

Monday to Sunday from 10.00am to 5.30pm. Mid-March to mid-November only.

GETTING THERE:

Shanklin is on the A3020 A 3055 roads. Parking is limited in the area.

Jireh House

St James's Square Yarmouth
Telephone: (01983) 760513

The setting is a lovely old house-once the town hall-in a handsome square close to the sea. For the traveller who feels overwhelmed by the scale and speed of bigger towns and wishes to take tea in an atmosphere of easy camaraderie, few places could be more appropriate than this nonchalant, friendly establishment in Yarmouth.

What to see:

This part of the island and its superb coastline are unspoilt (much of it belonging to the National Trust). Yarmouth is one of the prettiest towns on the island, with many 17th- and 18th-century buildings, and it is a sailing centre too. The area offers the visitor scenic walks, sandy beaches, pretty villages stately homes and much more besides.

The Old Thatch Tea Shop

Old Village, Shanklin
Telephone: (01983) 863184

The sun drifts into the cottage lighting up the intriguing little corners. After a day on the beach or in the town, the Old Thatch glows in the warmth of the afternoon. Inside, fine food and good company await. This is tea as we dream of it – gentle and welcoming to all.

What to see:

Shanklin has good beaches and a lovely chine (ravine) running down to the sea with a 45ft waterfall. There is a heritage centre which gives details of rare plants, nature trails and life in the area during Victorian times. In May and June, the south of the island can be the sunniest place in Britain.

Kisses and favours are sweet things.

Bartley Mill

Bell's Yew Green, Frant
Telephone: (01892) 890372

The tea room itself is famously comfortable, spread over two large rooms filled with old books and assorted bits and pieces. The real eye-catcher though is the window in the floor which reveals the mill wheel turning below. Weather permitting, enjoy tea in the peaceful, romantic garden overlooking the pond.

What to see:

A myth has grown up around the church in Frant. During restoration work in the last century, three men accidentally opened a tomb revealing the remains of a young woman who had died on her wedding day and been buried in her bridal dress. The curse of death had been decreed on any who disturbed her grave. Within the year the rector and the two restorers, who were present at the opening, were dead.

THE TEA:

The milled flour is used in the traditional and unusual range of cakes, scones and breads. Home cooked snacks and other specials are frequently on the menu. Price: from £3.50.

OPEN:

Daily from 10.00am to 5.00pm summer opening. Saturday and Sunday 10.00am to 5.00pm in winter.

GETTING THERE:

Bell's Yew Green is east of Frant on the B2169. Nearest motorway M25. Own car park.

Little strokes fell great oaks.

Butcher's Mere

Collier Street, near Marden
Telephone: (01892) 730495

In summertime, Butcher's Mere comes into its own. Afternoon tea is a delight, sitting in the garden, watching the geese on the large pond the banks of which are planted with herbs and willows. On cooler days tea is served in the cottage.

What to see:

Travel down to the village of Lamberhurst, it has retained much of its character and is worth a visit. Close by is Scotney Old Castle, part medieval tower and part ruined Tudor manor. Surrounded by a moat and set in beautiful gardens it is open (gardens only) at certain times of the year.

THE TEA:

The teas have well risen scones, home-made preserves and an array of cakes including coffee and chocolate, not to mention superb meringues. Indian, China, fruit and herbal teas are available. Diabetic tea also served. Price: set tea from £3.50.

OPEN:

Daily 10.00am to 7.00pm, Thursday from 2.00pm. Closed Christmas week and New Year.

GETTING THERE:

Collier Street is on the B2162. Nearest motorway M20. Own car park.

The bread never falls but on its buttered side.

HONOR BLACKMAN

Dear Mrs. Cross

Briefly - I know that all
sorts of other drinks are better for
me than tea. since tea is a stimulant
but there are occasions - especially
stressful ones - When nothing else
will serve.

Yours sincerely

Honor Blackman

Cherry Trees Tea Gallery/Garden

Matfield, near Tonbridge
Telephone: (01892) 722187

There are some tea rooms which immediately have a good feel about them and somehow you know that you are in for an enjoyable afternoon. Cherry Trees is one such place, presided over by Betty. On entering, the entire place is full of antiques and bric-a-brac that must have taken years to collect. Saturday 9.00am to 12.30pm and 3.00 to 6.00pm. Closed winter afternoons. Sunday 3.00 to 6.00pm.
What to see:
Matfield is the village where 'Mr Magika' the TV series was filmed. Nearby is Goudhurst a steep and charming village of former weavers' cottages, well worth exploring.

THE TEA:
The two set teas are cheerful and robust. The Kentish tea, hot toasted teacake, home-made cakes and a pot of tea is brought to your table in a selection of antique china. Price: £3.

OPEN:
Monday to Friday 9.00am to 1.00pm, 2.00 to 5.30pm. Closed Wednesday afternoon (winter).

GETTING THERE:
Signposted on the B2160. Ample parking.

A good name keeps it in the dark.

Cherubs

8 Potter Street, Sandwich
Telephone: (01304) 614805

Feel lucky if you chance upon this small elegant tea room, hidden half way along a street of old cottages and houses. The decor is refreshing with many personal touches, and the welcome is warm and attentive.
What to see:
Sandwich is an interesting town best explored on foot. It was once one of the most important naval bases in England, and one of the original Cinque ports. The town dates from Anglo-Saxon times but is rich in 16th- and 17th-century buildings. There are several excellent golf courses in the Sandwich area.

THE TEA:
The menu is small but varied allowing for choice. Sandwiches are made to order, scones are just out of the oven, and there are always five or six very tempting cakes. Tea choices include Indian, China and organic. Price: from £3.

OPEN:
Monday to Saturday 10.00am to 5.00pm. Closed on Sunday.

GETTING THERE:
Sandwich is off the A256, A257 and A258 roads. Nearest motorway M2. Town car parks.

Better some of the pudding than none of the pie.

THE TEA:

There is something to suit all appetites, and whether it's a scone tea, or just a slice of ginger cake you want, you can be sure the food will be fresh and the prices reasonable.

OPEN:

Daily 10.00am to 5.00pm. Closed over Christmas.

GETTING THERE:

Chilham is five miles to the south-west of Canterbury on the A252. Parking is permitted in the village.

Ask much to have a little.

THE TEA:

The choice is tempting, sandwiches, scones, shortbread and a splendid range of cakes including a flavoursome Cointreau special. There is a selection of teas. Price: from £3.

OPEN:

Tuesday to Sunday 10.30am to 5.30pm. Closed Monday except Bank Holidays and Christmas to New Year.

GETTING THERE:

Biddenden is on the A262 and A274 roads. Nearest motorways M20 and M25. Parking in the village.

The Copper Kettle

Chilham
Telephone: (01227) 730303

Of Kent's many Down and Wealden villages Chilham is one of the prettiest. On one side of the square stands the Copper Kettle. Inside, everything is in keeping with the style of the ancient house; low ceilings with copper pots hanging from the beams, small paned windows and old brick fireplaces.

What to see:

The church of St Mary is interesting; all that remains of the castle is the keep but the grounds are open to the public. The road from Chartham (three miles north-east) along the Chartham Downs gives some of the most beautiful views in Kent.

Claris's

1-3 High Street, Biddenden
Telephone: (01580) 291025

Claris's Tea Room and Craft Shop, both delightfully traditional, overlook the quaint main street of Biddenden, lined with timber and brick houses. The owners take genuine pride in the home baking and assortment of teas offered in their cosy establishment. Take time to browse in the adjoining craft shop – crammed with a variety of hand made goods.

What to see:

The village legend concerns 12th-century Siamese twins, Eliza and Mary Chulkhurst, who began the custom of distributing bread and cheese to the poor. The 15th-century church contains some unusual brasses.

They who live longest, see most.

Elan Arts Centre

Ide Hill, Sevenoaks
Telephone: (01732) 750344

No longer the village store, this 19th-century house is now a busy, bustling arts and crafts centre. Come to seek out some unusual presents or just treat yourself from an original selection of quality crafts and gifts. Temptation lies also in the delightful tea house with its changing varieties of home-baking. In the summer months an hour, or two, can be pleasantly whiled away, sipping tea, in the shade of the trees in the small garden.

What to see:
All around are the pretty villages, ancient churches, and the rural views typical of Kent, 'the garden of England'. Seaside resorts and the historic Cinque ports are easily reached by car.

THE TEA:
A good choice of cakes is always available, and several varieties of scone are also on the menu, including walnut and ginger with jam and cream. Tea or lemon tea is served. Prices are very reasonable.

OPEN:
Wednesday to Sunday 10.00am to 5.30pm, including Bank Holidays. Closed Monday, Tuesday, the month of January, and 2 weeks in February.

GETTING THERE:
Ide Hill lies south-west of Sevenoaks and is signposted off the B2042. Parking is permitted in the village.

As welcome as flowers in May.

Fir Tree House Tea Rooms

Penshurst, Tonbridge
Telephone: (01892) 870382

Penshurst is one of the prettiest villages in Kent, with historic houses and half-timbered cottages: amongst them is Fir Tree House. Inside, the old stone walls, oak beams and working fireplaces give the place an atmosphere of charm and goodwill. In warmer months, the English country garden, is draped in a soft haze as guests wander in, find a table, and settle down for a spot of tea!

What to see:
The village of Penshurst has a wealth of half-timbered cottages and a medieval church, but the finest building in the village is Penshurst Place, a magnificent house, with a beautiful formal garden.

THE TEA:
The afternoon tea of granary bread, scones and cakes is full of flavour and priced at £3. The tea menu has plenty of other choices.

OPEN:
April to October: Tuesday to Sunday 1.30 to 5.30pm, closed Monday. January to Easter: Saturday and Sunday only 1.30 to 5.30pm. Closed for the months of November and December.

GETTING THERE:
Penshurst is five miles north-east of Tunbridge Wells on the B2176. Parking is possible in the village.

A hedge between keeps friendship green.

Peggoty's Tea Shoppe

122 High Street, Tenterden
Telephone: (0158076) 4393

A good address to know when visiting Tenterden or the surrounding area, when you're in the mood for a light bite and a pot of tea. In good weather, tables trickle out onto the pavement, while inside tea is sipped beneath beamed ceilings in an old world atmosphere. This is simple traditional tea fare, nothing too fancy but generally satisfying. Service is friendly and quick, and comes with a smile.

What to see:

Tenterden is a charming unspoilt market town, famous for its wide, tree-lined high street. Well worth a visit are St Mildred's Church and the local museum.

THE TEA:

In addition to the set cream tea, assorted scones and cakes are a speciality. A choice of seventeen teas includes Indian, China, Ceylon, herbal and fruit. Prices are very reasonable, from £4.

OPEN:

Monday to Saturday 10.00am to 5.00pm. Sunday 2.00 to 6.00pm. Closed Wednesday and Sunday morning.

GETTING THERE:

Tenterden is situated on the main A28. Parking permitted up to two hours in designated spaces.

Share and share alike.

Queen Elizabeth's Guest Chamber

High Street, Canterbury
Telephone: (01227) 464080

If wondering about the name of this tea place, in an ancient black and white building, the answer lies herein: in 1573 Queen Elizabeth I entertained a French royal guest – The Duke of Alençon – with a view to a possible marriage. The interior is still striking, with ancient floors and a particularly decorative ceiling – unchanged since 1573.

What to see:

It is, of course, the cathedral which brings most people to Canterbury, one of Britain's finest and most interesting, with many historical associations. It is the site of Thomas à Becket's martydom, and houses the tomb of the Black Prince and much more. In a vault in St Dunstan's Church lies the severed head of St Thomas Moore.

THE TEA:

The tea menu, from 2.30pm onwards, offers set teas and individual items such as cakes and pastries baked on the premises. A choice of teas is offered. Price: from £3.

OPEN:

Monday to Sunday 10.00am to 5.30pm.

GETTING THERE:

Canterbury is on the A2/M2 route. Parking in town car parks only.

Great hopes make great men.

Roses

High Street, St Margaret's at Cliffe
Telephone: (01304) 852126

Roses is a pretty little tea shop that offers a small but carefully chosen selection of interesting and unusual antiques. The atmosphere is cosy and welcoming and on sunny days tea in the garden is not to be hurried over, so bring a friend.

What to see:
Finds include a small local area museum and The Pines, a secluded garden with a waterfall and a statue of Winston Churchill. Discover also, pathways which run alongside the famous White Cliffs. Further along are the towns of Walmer and Deal – both with castles.

The Sentry Box Tea Rooms

8 The Street, Appledore
Telephone: (01233) 758272

From the tea room, one looks across a main village street with houses of various styles and ages, from the 16th century onwards, harmoniously mixed. Inside you'll find unusual beams and fireplaces and the old walls making a good background for family photographs and collections of militaria that are on display. The area around Appledore is steeped in ancient and modern military history and is what gives the Sentry Box its name!

What to see:
The village itself with its attractive mix of houses. The church of St Peter and St Paul was rebuilt in 1380 having been burnt down by the French!

---

*Take time when time comes,
lest time steal away.*

THE TEA:
Buttery scones, tangy lemon sponge and superb chocolate cake are all equally delicious. There is a small choice of teas. Price: from £2.

OPEN:
Tuesday to Sunday 10.30am to 5.00pm. Closed Sunday and Monday except Bank Holidays. Sunday open 12.00 to 5pm in Summer months.

GETTING THERE:
St Margaret's at Cliffe is three miles from Dover off the A258. Nearest motorway M20. Own car park.

Hunger increases the understanding.

THE TEA:
Most popular is the set high tea. For just £2.50 you are offered a fresh boiled egg, brown bread and butter, a slice of fruit cake or a scone, butter and jam, with a pot of tea. But there are plenty of other choices.

OPEN:
Monday to Saturday 10.30am to 5.00pm, Sunday 11.00am to 6.00pm.

GETTING THERE:
Appledore is to the north-east of Rye on the B2080. Parking for cars is available in the village.

THE TEA:
The menu is simple and satisfying offering savoury dishes and flavoursome baking. There are always home-made scones and a choice of cakes, served with a selection of tea blends. Price: from £2.50. (Counter service).

OPEN:
Tuesday to Sunday 12 to 5.30pm. Closed Monday. October to December restricted opening, please check.

GETTING THERE:
Sissinghurst is east of Tunbridge Wells on the A262. Nearest motorways M20 and M25. Own car park.

———◇———

Nature is conquered by obeying her.

———◇———

Sissinghurst Granary

Sissinghurst Castle Garden, near Cranbrook
Telephone: (01580) 715330

The old granary has been restored and turned into a charming, rustic tea room. It is an attractive and airy setting for tea, full of the natural colours of brick and wood. A table by the window reveals fine views of the beautiful gardens.

What to see:
The most famous house in the area is Sissinghurst Castle. It was virtually a ruin when Vita Sackville-West and her husband, Harold Nicholson, rescued it in 1930. The gardens were planned as a series of intimate areas and are visited by thousands of people every year. The village of Sissinghurst contains many of the old Kentish white, weather-board houses.

———◇———

THE TEA:
Good cakes and pastries include gingerbread, fruit tarts, pineapple torte, date and walnut or banana bread, complemented by a range of tea blends such as Indian, China and herbal. Price: set tea from £3.40.

OPEN:
Tuesday to Saturday 10.00am to 4.30pm. Closed Sunday and Monday.

GETTING THERE:
Borough Green is on the A25. Nearest motorways M20 and M25. Parking in the village.

The Tea House

17 High Street, Borough Green
Telephone: (01732) 883073

If you're looking for a genuine local meeting place, full of satisfied customers, this is it. The Tea House is an inviting spot, where the owner keeps careful tabs on the two charming rooms to make sure everyone is well served.

What to see:
South of the village of Ightham is Ightham Mote. Built in the 14th century it is one of the few remaining moated houses in England. It derives its name, not from the moat, but from the 'moot' or council which convened here in medieval times. Check opening times. Near the centre of the village on a little hill stands St Peter's Church, dating from the 14th century.

———◇———

Plenty makes dainty.

———◇———

Tiffins

The Green, Westerham
Telephone: (01959) 562564

Westerham, very much a Wealden town, has been inhabited since the very earliest times. Today houses of the 18th and 19th centuries flank the main streets and the village green, and it's on the edge of the green you'll discover Tiffins. Wander inside and you'll find an attractive tea room in which the aromas of loose-leaf teas and English fruit cake mingle with the soothing sounds of classical music.

What to see:
On the green are statues of General Wolfe and Sir Winston Churchill, the two most famous local residents. Both Quebec House, where General Wolfe spent his childhood, and Chartwell, Winston Churchill's home, are open to the public.

The Village Tea Shop

Chiddingstone
Telephone: (01892) 870326

Many famous people have lived in the village of Chiddingstone, one of the best known was Sir Thomas Bullen, father of Anne Bullen (Boleyn). He purchased Burghersh Court in 1517 and it is within the Old Coach House that you'll discover the tea shop. The style of the place is simplicity itself, decorated in creams and browns and opening out onto a flower filled courtyard.

What to see:
Chiddingstone is a single street village lined with old half-timbered houses. It contains a 19th-century house known as Chiddingstone Castle – open to the public at certain times. Nearby is the 'Chiding Stone' used to subdue nagging wives!

THE TEA:
The small tea menu changes frequently but may include open sandwiches, teabreads, scones with clotted cream and imaginative fruit and sponge cakes. There is a good selection of loose-leaf teas. Price: from £3.50.

OPEN:
Tuesday to Friday 10.00am to 5.15pm, Saturday 10.00am to 5.30pm, Sunday and Monday 2.30 to 5.30pm.

GETTING THERE:
Can be approached from the A223 and the A25. Parking is permitted in the village.

Everything is good in its season.

THE TEA:
Recommended are the scones, teacakes, and apple cakes, which are all home-baked. Also offered is a selection of herbal and speciality teas. A creamed tea is priced at £3.

OPEN:
Tuesday to Sunday 11.00am to 5.30pm. Closed Monday.

GETTING THERE:
Chiddingstone is off the B2027 Edenbridge to Tonbridge road. Nearest motorway M25. Ample parking in the village.

As they brew so let them drink.

Maureen Lipman

Dear Patricia,

Thank you very much for your letter and for the appreciative comments on the books and the play.

The Tea Dance

We were ushered to our white linen-covered table, boasting fine china and fresh flowers, by a smiling courteous maitre d', and presented with the menu. High tea is not a low price but I'm convinced you get what you pay for. Personally, I could hardly find my chair let alone choose my choux because the dance floor entertainment was so mesmerising

The Waldorf Tea Dance was a whole new ballroom. In fact I'd go as far as to say that all human life was there, if you knew how to look and you looked with affection and without malice.

Best wishes,

Gainsborough Old Hall

Gainsborough
Telephone: (01427) 612669

Enjoying a visit to a stately home and indulging in tea, always seem to go together. The Hall in Gainsborough provides the perfect opportunity to do both. A day here will quieten the nerve endings and soothe the fevered brow. The tea room is situated in the Lower Inner chamber, where light refreshments and home-made goodies are served.

What to see:

Although parts of Lincolnshire can be flat, its coast and nature reserves make it a great place for drivers, walkers and birdwatchers. Gainsborough was the basis for 'St Ogg's' in 'Mill on the Floss' by George Eliot, and The Hall itself has a fascinating history.

THE TEA:

The ladies who serve are also the ladies who bake! There is nothing over-fussy or elaborate just moist teabreads, honey sponges and wholesome scones served with pots of tea. Price from £3.

OPEN:

Monday to Saturday from 10.00am to 5.00pm. Sunday 2-5.00pm. Closed Sundays November to Easter.

GETTING THERE:

Gainsborough is on the A631 and A156 roads. Nearest motorway M1. Parking in the town.

Today is the scholar of yesterday.

The George of Stamford

71 St Martin's
Telephone: (01780) 55171

The George, a beautiful 16th-century coaching inn, retains the enchantment of its long history. At the heart of the hotel is an atmospheric lounge with a log fire that crackles and blazes on chilly afternoons. It is sometimes used for toasting muffins or warming scones at tea time.

What to see:

Stamford, a medieval town built in the local, mellow Collyweston stone, is full of interest with at least six churches, many narrow lanes and streets lined with Queen Anne and Georgian mansions. It is the most delightful place to explore on foot. Daniel Lambert, the fattest Englishman ever, and Sir Malcolm Sargent the renowned conductor are both buried in Stamford.

THE TEA:

The tea menu offers the lightest of scones and a selection of traditional English cakes served with a choice of excellent teas. Price: from £4.

OPEN:

Monday to Sunday 3.30 to 5.30pm. Throughout the year.

GETTING THERE:

Stamford is on the A1 Grantham road. Own car park. Parking in the town, free and pay and display.

As true as the dial to the sun.

THE TEA:

Baking is without doubt the little tea room's forte. The cakes and sponges ooze with delicious fillings and sandwiches, soups and hot lunches also emerge from the kitchen. This is real food made and served by hardworking, friendly people. Price: from £3.50.

OPEN:

Tuesday to Sunday from 10.30am to 4.30pm. Closed Monday.

GETTING THERE:

Horncastle is on the A153 A158 roads. Free parking in the town car park.

There is a good time coming.

THE TEA:

The dining room offers standard fare and various set teas, such as, high and toasted. The teas are good, Darjeeling, with a mild flavour, and Lapsang, rich and smoky, to name but two. Price: from £3.50.

OPEN:

Monday to Saturday from 10.00am to 5.00pm. Tea is served from 2.00pm onwards. Closed Sunday.

GETTING THERE:

Lincoln is on the A15, A46 A158 roads. Nearest motorways M1 and M180. Restricted parking.

Needles & Nosh

36, West Street Horncastle
Telephone: (01507) 522 687

Paradise is chancing upon a place such as Needles and Nosh. It has considerable charm. The dining room is a small low-ceilinged room busily decorated with hand-made crafts and personal treasures. Elsewhere on the same floor is another room for use on busier days.

What to see:

Lincolnshire is probably one of the least known and least explored counties in England. Yet it has its own distinctive scenery and attractive towns and villages, if the traveller has the patience to seek them out. When you have explored the Wolds, recognised as an area of outstanding beauty, there is always Lincoln, coastal resorts such as Skegness and some fine old castles and mansions to look at.

Stokes

High Street Lincoln
Telephone: (01522) 513825

This stunning black-and-white building is perched on a medieval bridge which spans the River Witham in the heart of Lincoln. The ground floor emporium sells teas and coffees whilst upstairs the snug rooms have low ceilings and traditional furniture. Through small leaded windows are views of the water, boats and the occasional swan.

What to see:

Lincoln has many sights to interest the visitor. The cathedral and castle sit on top of a 200-foot ridge and from there narrow streets of medieval houses wend their way down into the town. There are museums and galleries and riverside and canal walks. All around the city are, the rolling Wolds and the contrasting flat fens.

What has been may be again.

Tealby Tea Rooms

Tealby
Telephone: (01673) 838261

In the heart of the village this bright, bustling tea room is very popular with locals and visitors alike. A hundred years ago this was a meeting place for tea and the formula, then as now, remains the same: a pleasant ambience, good value and a consistent standard of baking. People happily come for such delights.

What to see:

The village is often regarded as one of the prettiest in the county, with its old cottages, three fords and the Viking-Way passing through it. The vast county of Lincolnshire is an acquired taste but has villages, scenery and a coastline as distinctive as any. An added bonus is that paths and roads are seldom crowded even in high season.

THE TEA:

Set teas, including a cream and a 'high tea' are always popular. Cakes to get the taste buds buzzing include chocolate fudge and carrot cake, but the cream gateaux also get a yes-vote. Choices of tea available. Price; from £3.

OPEN:

Tuesday to Sunday and Bank Holiday Mondays 10.30 to 5.30pm. April to September. Winter months, weekends only.

GETTING THERE:

Tealby is east of Market Rasen on the B1203. Parking in the village.

Names and nature do often agree.

London N3

College Farm, The Tea House

Fitzalan Road
Telephone: (0181) 349 0690

For a touch of country living in London, make your way to College Farm; it's great fun to discover and makes an unusual day out, with plenty to see, including rare breeds of animals. The old dairy, where tea is served, was built in 1864 and became a tea house in 1925. For many years, however, it was neglected, until restore, and the tea tradition revived. The atmospheric setting – blue and white Minton wall tiles, lace tablecloths, old napkins, blue and white china and many other personal touches – makes it very special.

What to see:

The farm is interesting and well worth a visit. There is an open day on the first Sunday of every month with many special events. Small entrance charge.

THE TEA:

Home-made scones, luscious clotted cream and a choice of home-made preserves served with a variety of teas. Price: from £3.

OPEN:

Saturday, Sunday and Bank Holiday Mondays 2.30 to 5.30pm.

GETTING THERE:

Nearest tube Finchley Central, then a walk or a bus. Easy to find by car and there's street parking.

Love lives in cottages as well as in courts.

The tea:

Two set teas: a cream tea price £3.90 or a high tea £4.80. Then there's always a slice of home-made cake. Teas served include Assam, Darjeeling, Earl Grey and a variety of fruit and herb tisanes.

OPEN:

Tuesday to Friday 11.30am to 6.00pm, Saturday from 10.00am, Sunday, 11.00am to 6.00pm. Closed Monday.

GETTING THERE:

By bus to Crouch End Broadway. Parking is possible.

The mere chink of cups and saucers tunes the mind to happy repose.
– Anon

The Wisteria Tea Rooms

14 Middle Lane
Telephone: (0181) 348 2669

Tucked away in coolest Crouch End, The Wisteria Tea Rooms are a sheer delight, just gazing in through the window fills you with nostalgia – chintz wallpaper, period prints and pictures with plenty of Victorian bric-a-brac, much of which is for sale. Tables are covered with lace tablecloths and there is seating for two, four or eight. On warm days take tea in the pretty garden. Strictly no smoking.

What to see:

The first television broadcasts were sent out from Alexandra Palace in 1936, it is well worth a visit, as is the five-hundred acre park. It plays host to numerous events throughout the year.

The tea:

There's no set tea, but tea and a range of freshly baked cakes are available throughout the day, including hazelnut cake, cheesecake and apple tart. Teas served include Indian, China and herbal. Price: around £3.

OPEN:

Monday to Saturday 8.30am to 9.00pm, Sunday 9.30am to 9.00pm (later in summer).

GETTING THERE:

Nearest tube Chalk Farm then a walk, or British Rail to Primrose Hill. Parking is possible!

London NW1

The Primrose Patisserie

136 Regent's Park Road
Telephone: (0171) 722 7848

A nearby, small green hill gives this tea room its name, The Primrose. Built in Victorian times, it still retains some period characteristics of that era and is simply but pleasantly furnished. After walking over the hill, tea is just moments away.

What to see:

Regent's Park, which began as part of Henry VIII's hunting forest contains an open air theatre, a lake for waterfowl and boating, Queen Mary's Rose Garden and The London Zoo.

A maid that laughs is half taken.

Burgh House

New End Square
Telephone: (0171) 431 0144

Burgh House, with many famous associations and its fair share of historic involvement, is a centre for concerts and exhibitions, with a local history museum and buttery. Installed in the former kitchens and servants' quarters is the Burgh Buttery. It's a modest spot where regulars and visitors like to meet and eat, enjoying the simple 'take us as you find us' atmosphere.

What to see:
Hampstead and its Heath, standing on a hill to the north of London has an identity all its own which is reflected in the many famous people who have chosen to live there over the years. It is interesting to explore the many charming side streets.

THE TEA:
Amongst the cluster of cakes at the counter are sponges, scones, gateaux and fruit tarts, all are worth sampling! Indian and herbal are the tea choices. Price: from £3.

OPEN:
The House: 12 noon to 5.00pm, the Buttery: 11.00am to 5.30pm Wednesday to Sunday.

GETTING THERE:
Nearest tube Hampstead, then a walk through the charming backstreets of the area. Parking is possible

What has been may be.

The Hampstead Tea Rooms

9 Southend Road
Telephone: (0171) 435 9563

Can you jog or even walk past the Hampstead Tea Rooms without stopping to marvel at the endless rows of enticing pastries? Once you've paused you will soon find your way inside for a spot of tea. There are three small, intimate seating areas, and in good weather sit outside and watch the busy Hampstead world pass by.
A choice of teas includes Indian, Earl Grey and several herbal infusions.

What to see:
Close by is the Keats Memorial House containing many personal relics of the poet. Walk over Hampstead Heath and see the ponds and the wonderful view over London.

The things of friends are in common.

THE TEA:
A set tea of scones, preserve and cream with tea costs £3. The scones are plump and tender and baked on the premises. There's also a marvellous selection of pastries which even the most hardened will find irresistible.

OPEN:
Monday to Saturday 9.00am to 7.00pm, Sunday 9.30am to 7.00pm.

GETTING THERE:
Nearest tube Belsize Park, but it's a fair distance. British Rail North London line is closest. Parking is possible.

THE TEA:
The menu offers some twenty different varieties of cakes and tarts, as well as scones and fresh rolls and bread. A pot of tea and a pastry costs around £3.50.

OPEN:
Daily 9.00am to 6.00pm, throughout the year.

GETTING THERE:
The nearest tube is Hampstead. Parking is possible in the side streets.

A little labour, much health.

THE TEA:
The stone walls, high ceiling and stained glass windows of the church make an atmospheric setting for a cup of tea and a slice of cake. On warm days sit in the peaceful garden. Price: from £2.50.

OPEN:
Monday to Friday 10.30am to 4.00pm. Sunday 10.30am to 5.00pm. Closed Saturday, and three months from the second Sunday in December to the first Sunday in March. Admission free.

GETTING THERE:
Nearest tube station Vauxhall. Meter parking in the area.

Louis Patisserie

32 Heath Street
Telephone: (0171) 435 9908

A diminutive shop on one of Hampstead's most lively village streets. Like taking a trip to old Vienna or Budapest, Louis Patisserie is sheer indulgence. All year round, the window tempts passers-by with marzipan confections, apple strudels, chocolate and cream delights and dark chocolate Linzertortes! They can all be sampled in the little tea salon at the back of the shop.

What to see:
Hampstead has an interesting selection of small shops, pubs and restaurants. A long walk up Heath Street and past the pond eventually leads to the Heath, over 800 acres of park and woodland beloved by families, walkers, picnickers and those just wishing to enjoy the open space.

London SE1
Museum of Garden History

St Mary-at-Lambeth, Lambeth Palace Road
Telephone: (0171) 261 1891

The Tradescant Trust, Patron HRH The Prince of Wales, was established for two reasons: firstly to save the historic church of St Mary-at-Lambeth from demolition and secondly to found the first Museum of Garden History.

What to see:
There were two John Tradescants, father and son, gardeners successively to Lord Salisbury, the Duke of Buckingham and Charles I. They are both buried in a fine tomb, next to that of Admiral Bligh of the 'Bounty', in the churchyard.

*This rule in gardening never forget,
to sow dry and to set wet.*

Peter de Wit (Toymaker)

21 Greenwich Church Street
Telephone: (0181) 305 0048

The objects and toys in this little shop window are so colourful, people can't help but stop and look. The owners specialise in making unique wooden toys and hand painted furniture items. If there's time – and a table free – do stop for tea and a slice of home-made apple and blackberry pie. In good weather one can relax on the small outdoor terrace.

What to see:

Of special interest are: The National Maritime Museum, The Old Royal Observatory, The Royal Naval College and The 'Cutty Sark', the last tea clipper.

A ship and a woman are ever repairing.

THE TEA:

A cream tea of scones, Cornish clotted cream and home-made strawberry conserve will keep you going through the afternoon, price from £3.50. A pot of tea and a slice of cake from £2.

OPEN:

Tuesday to Friday from 10.00am to 5.00pm. Weekends from 10.00am to 7.00pm.

GETTING THERE:

By boat, from Charing Cross pier. By docklands light railway to Island Gardens then a walk through the Greenwich foot tunnel. By car on the A102. Parking is limited.

London SW1

The Lanesborough

Hyde Park Corner
Telephone: (0171) 259 5599

You simply can't beat the location of this luxurious hotel. It is but a few blocks from Buckingham Palace, major shopping, theatres and restaurants. It's a surprise to discover it was originally a London hospital-Saint George's. The Conservatory, under a huge glass cupola, amid triffid-like potted palms is the place for a refined and stylish tea.

What to see:

Almost opposite the hotel is Apsley House, built in the 1770's and bought by the Duke of Wellington in 1817. It contains good collections of china, furniture, paintings and a trove of Napoleonic war bounty. Buckingham Palace, the London residence of the Queen, is now open during the months of August and September for viewing of the State Apartments.

THE TEA:

One would expect an excellent serving of afternoon tea, and the Lanesborough does not disappoint. Throw your cares into a corner, forget the real world, and enjoy every minute. Price: from £14.50.

OPEN:

Daily from 3.30-6.00pm. Smart dress advised. Booking not always necessary.

GETTING THERE:

Nearest tube is Hyde Park Corner. Many buses travel to the area. Meter parking only.

A thing learned now is a habit for life.

87

TEA-TOTAL

I HAVE TO DECLARE: TAKING SOME SATISFACTION FROM THE NATIONAL SHRIEK OF HORROR — THAT TEA HAS NEVER MEANT MUCH TO ME. AS A CHILD, I DRANK IT BECAUSE IT WAS THE ONLY HOT DRINK GENERALLY AVAILABLE.

I COULD NEVER UNDERSTAND THE OBSESSION WITH IT, SIMPLY COULD NOT TOLERATE THE SMUG SMIRK OF THE CONGENITAL TEA-DRINKER, CROONING 'LET'S HAVE A CUPPA TEA!' AS IF THAT WERE SOME ARCANE SOLUTION TO ALL THE TROUBLES OF THE WORLD, THE CURE FOR ALL OF NATURE'S ILLS. NOR COULD I BEAR THE OTHER PRIGGISH PLEA: 'LET'S PUT THE KETTLE ON!' AS IF A SPOUTED TIN-CAN CONTAINED SOME VERY GREAT AND SPECIAL SECRET THAT ONLY A TRUE BRIT COULD SHARE. EVEN TO THIS DAY, I CANNOT STOMACH THE WORD: 'BREW!'

ONCE I HAD DISCOVERED IT, I GLEEFULLY DRANK COFFEE, THEN INSTANT COFFEE, THEN INSTANT DECAFFEINATED COFFEE, ENJOYING EVERY VENGEFUL SIP. UNTIL I DISCOVERED HERBAL TEA.

THERE WAS SOMETHING REFRESHING ABOUT THE IDEA OF THE FRUIT, THE FACT THAT IT DID NOT CONTAIN ANY DRUG, DID NOT NEED THE FATTENING INDULGENCES OF MILK OR SUGAR.

AND WITH NAMES LIKE 'ORANGE DAZZLER', 'MIXED FRUIT', AND 'BLACKCURRANT BRACER', AND INGREDIENTS LIKE HIBISCUS, ROSEHIPS, CINNAMON BARK, MALLOW LEAVES AND LEMON GRASS, WHO COULD RESIST THE CALL TO 'PUT THE KETTLE ON!' AND 'LET'S HAVE A CUPPA HERBAL TEA!'

Good luck with the book,

Ron Moody

Harrods

Knightsbridge
Telephone: (0171) 730 1234

This famous store in the heart of Knightsbridge, where you could spend hours just looking around, serves delicious afternoon teas. Take tea on the terrace, or in the Georgian restaurant – both are good places for taking the family.

What to see:

Harrods is one of the largest and most famous stores in the world. In the vast terracotta building it is possible to buy just about anything on earth and to spend an entire day without seeing it all.

The quickest way to know a woman is to go shopping with her. – Marcelene Cox

---

The Hyde Park Hotel

Knightsbridge
Telephone: (0171) 235 2000

The Park Room has been restored to its former glory – blues, ivory and gold abound in this most elegant of rooms. The view, if you're fortunate enough to be seated by the window, is over Hyde Park and Rotten Row. It is well known that the Queen Mother used to accompany the young princesses to the Park Room for afternoon tea – as a special treat. Set aside plenty of time to treat yourself!

What to see:

There are an enormous variety of shops in the area, from department store to exclusive designer outlets. Further along at South Kensington are the Victoria and Albert, Natural History and Science Museums.

He that trusts much, obliges much.

THE TEA:

On the terrace the set tea is £10: a tasty selection of sandwiches, served on brown bread, scones complete with preserve and cream, and an assortment of pastries. Teas served include Earl Grey, Indian and herbal. A full afternoon tea is also served in the Georgian Restaurant. Price from £11.50.

OPEN:

Monday to Saturday 3.30 to 5.30pm for tea. The store is open from 9.30am to 6.00pm.

GETTING THERE:

Nearest tube Knightsbridge, many buses travel to the area. Harrods has its own car park, otherwise meter parking.

THE TEA:

Price from £13.50 for assorted sandwiches, toasted English muffins, scones, with Devonshire cream and jam and a varied choice of cakes and pastries. Teas served include Indian, China and Russian.

OPEN:

Monday to Friday 4.00 to 6.00pm, Saturday and Sunday 4.00 to 6.00pm.

GETTING THERE:

Nearest tube Knightsbridge, numerous buses travel to the area. Monday to Saturday meter parking. Free parking on Sunday

89

THE TEA:
On Wednesdays, tea and biscuits. On Sundays home-made scones with jam, or slices of fruit cake served with cups of well made Indian tea. Don't be late as the scones go very quickly. Price: all items are from around £1.

OPEN:
April to the middle of October: Wednesday and Sunday only, 2.00 to 5.00pm. There is an entrance charge.

GETTING THERE:
Nearest tube Sloane Square. Free parking in the western end of Battersea Park.

THE TEA:
Afternoon tea is handled with great care. The scones are tender and served with apple butter and cream-delicious with Earl Grey. It would be a pity not to partake of a slice of cake of the day. Price: from £5.

OPEN:
Monday to Saturday from 10.00am to 5.30pm for morning breaks and lunches. Tea served from 3.30pm onwards.

GETTING THERE:
Nearest tube, Knightsbridge. Meter parking in the area.

Who knows most forgives most.

Chelsea Physic Garden

66 Royal Hospital Road
Telephone: (0171) 352 5646

This is a truly remarkable corner of London. It must be among the oldest of original gardens planted in the capital. You will discover rare plants and trees growing here, as well as a rich variety of medicinal and culinary herbs. There are benches and seats everywhere, in the sun and under trees, for you to enjoy the garden.

What to see:
Chelsea Old Church (All Saints) has an interesting history. It contains the St Thomas More chapel.

Nature, time and patience are the three great physicians.

Emporia Armani

187, Brompton Road
Telephone: (0171) 823 8818

Any afternoon in deepest Knightsbridge, why not join the natives as they inspect the fashion on offer in the Armani emporium. Eventually all this shopaholic buzz will turn your thoughts towards, well, food, there is no need to make a hasty exit. Upstairs, there is a small, but perfectly formed, place to eat.

What to see:
The Victoria and Albert Museum, with seven miles of gallery space, has something to interest almost everyone. The collections of fine and applied art are the best in the world and in addition, there are many special activities such as, lectures, concerts and various talks. On Saturdays join the throng heading for Portobello market.

Richoux

86, Brompton Road
Telephone: (0171) 584 8300

Richoux rather cleverly catches the atmosphere of a superior drawing room with its polite waistcoated waiters, aproned waitresses, classical music and discreet furnishings. It's all very reassuring, and surely, the best time to eat cakes and crumpets is when you're completely relaxed.

What to see:
Kensington Palace, once a private town house was re-modelled by Sir Christopher Wren and then enlarged by William Kent. It was the birthplace of Queen Victoria. It is now the London residence of members of the present Royal Family. Treasures to be seen include furniture from the Royal Collection and the Court Dress Collection. Please check opening times.

THE TEA:
Individual pastries are brought to you on a platter, or choose what you desire from the display of cakes. The menu also offers two set teas accompanied by Indian, China, infusions and coffees. Price: from £5.

OPEN:
Daily from 8.30am to 8.00pm. Except Sunday, open from 10.00am.

GETTING THERE:
Nearest tube is Knightsbridge. Many buses travel to the area. Meter parking only.

One love expels another.

London SW4

Tea Time

The Pavement
Telephone: (0171) 622 4944

In a small parade of shops close to Clapham Common, this pleasant tea shop offers a good range of home-baking. Lloyd Loom chairs are complemented by green walls displaying pictures, and by lace covered tables in the downstairs room.

What to see:
Clapham has very little in the way of tourist attractions, its centre piece is the Common which stretches almost a mile from one side to the other. It is at its best in the autumn. There is a proliferation of health food and gift shops as well as pubs and restaurants.

THE TEA:
Two set teas are offered as well as a variety of home-made cakes. An extensive range of teas includes Indian, China, Ceylon and a choice of fruit or herbal tisanes. Price: from £6.95 for a tea time special.

OPEN:
Monday to Saturday 10.30am to 5.30pm, Sunday 10.00am to 6.00pm.

GETTING THERE:
Nearest tube Clapham North. Parking is possible.

Should I after tea and cakes and ices Have the strength to force the moment to its crisis.
– TS Eliot

THE TEA:
The menu offers fine and simple Russian and English fare, for breakfast, lunch and afternoon tea, and some of the best bakes and cakes in the area. Try the light sultana cheesecake-vatrouchka. Price: from £5.

OPEN:
Monday to Saturday from 9.00am to 7.00pm. Sunday open from 10.00am to 8.00pm.

GETTING THERE:
Nearest tube is Putney Bridge. There is parking in the side streets.

Speak and speed, ask and have.

Stravinsky's Russian Tea House

8, Fulham High Street
Telephone: (0171) 371 0001

Look around and you'll see table after table filled with couples, lone individuals and Mata Hari look-a-likes, sipping Russian tea, carefully perfecting the art of doing absolutely nothing. This is Stravinsky's, a Russian-inspired tea house that has grown up in this part of Fulham.

What to see:

The area from here to Sloane Square is bursting with interesting small, specialist shops and boutiques. The New King's road though is probably the biggest lure for a buying trip. The Royal Hospital, one of Christopher Wren's buildings, still houses the red-coated Chelsea pensioners.

THE TEA:
There are several set teas, choices of toasted sandwiches and light snacks. You will be offered an assortment of teas, as well as coffee and cold drinks. Price: set teas from £4.50.

OPEN:
Monday to Saturday tea served from 11.00am to 7.00pm. Dinner from 7-11.00pm. Sunday, brunch from 11.00am to 2.00pm. Teas from 2-7.00pm.

GETTING THERE:
Nearest tube Clapham Common then a walk or take a bus. Limited parking in the area.

London SW11
The Tea Gallery

103 Lavender Hill
Telephone: (0171) 350 2564

If a casual, cosmopolitan world is what attracts you, then steam ahead to this south London favourite. It's the kind of place you walk into, laugh, and feel immediately at home. Take its Eastern inspired decor or, is it mid-Clapham Gothic? It's odds-n-sods china and comfortable collection of tables and chairs and enjoy the world of familiar fare but with a few surprises.

What to see:

The commons, Clapham or Wandsworth are good for walking the dog. There are some interesting small shops in the area. Further afield are Dulwich College Picture Gallery in south east London, or Syon House and Osterley Park in west London.

Woman that cries hush bids kiss.

Natashas

Wiseton Road
Telephone: (0181) 767 5357

After a stroll across Wandsworth Common, linger over a pot of tea and a slice of home-made cake at this appealing tea room with its Lloyd Loom chairs and marble topped tables. In good weather tables are moved out on to the pavement.

What to see:
There is very little in the way of tourist attractions in Wandsworth. So take a stroll over the common, at its best in Autumn, or there are plenty of shops to browse around. Several times a year travelling circuses and fairs arrive at the commons – Clapham and Wandsworth.

THE TEA:
As well as two set teas, there is an excellent display of home-baking, including fruit slices, chocolate cake and exotic fruit tarts. Indian, China, Ceylon and herbal teas are available. Price: from £4.

OPEN:
Monday to Sunday 9.00am to 7.30pm. Throughout the year.

GETTING THERE:
British Rail to Wandsworth Common, many buses travel to the area. Parking is possible nearby.

It is good to be neither too high nor too low.

London SW19
Cannizaro House

West Side, Wimbledon Common
Telephone: (0181) 879 1464

Cannizaro is a fascinating Georgian jewel built in the early 18th century. The house derives its name from the late 19th-century owners, the Duke and Duchess of Cannizaro. Today the glory of the past intertwines with the comfort and style of the present, perfectly encapsulated by the taking of tea in the restaurant or, on warm days, on the terrace under a parasol.

What to see:
Wimbledon is one of London's most pleasant suburbs, with good shops and acres of parkland. For most people, however, the name Wimbledon, means one thing, and that is tennis. The tournament has been played here, annually, for over a hundred years.

THE TEA:
Price £10 for a full English tea. Home-made scones with clotted cream, triangles of mixed sandwiches and a selection of Cannizaro cakes. Teas include Indian, China, Ceylon and fruit blends.

OPEN:
Daily 3.00 to 5.00pm.

GETTING THERE:
Nearest tube Wimbledon, but a car is really most convenient. Own car park.

A good deed is never lost.

THE TEA:
Munch happily on scones with cream and jam or on freshly made sandwiches and slabs of chunky cakes. Good choices of teas, coffees and other hot and cold drinks. Price: from £4.50.

OPEN:
Daily from 8.00am to 7.00pm.

GETTING THERE:
Nearest tube is Wimbledon then a bus ride up to the village. Free parking around the common. Meter parking in the village.

Many a heart is caught in the rebound.

The Coffee Shop

High Street, Wimbledon
Telephone: (0181) 947 5341

The Coffee Shop, set in the heart of Wimbledon Village, does indeed serve afternoon teas, and is as popular as it is tiny. The staff are breezy, you can't dance a tango between the tables but it does lend itself either to friendly banter with the table next door or eavesdropping on the Wimbledon tea set.

What to see:
This corner of Wimbledon prides itself on its villageyness, and off the main street, filled with interesting small shops, are narrow lanes of picturesque houses. The common offers acres of open parkland. There are two theatres in the area, the Wimbledon, built in 1910, and the Polka with shows and puppet plays specifically for children.

THE TEA:
A first-class three-course tea of selected sandwiches, scones, clotted cream and strawberry preserve, and a well-chosen assortment of pastries, served with a range of teas including Claridge's own blend. Price from £15.50.

OPEN:
Daily 3.30 to 5.00pm throughout the year. Smart dress essential.

GETTING THERE:
Nearest tube Bond Street, then a wander through the streets of Mayfair. Meter parking.

London W1
Claridge's

Brook Street
Telephone: (0171) 629 8860

Claridge's brings together all the elegant qualities of an established English hotel. You enter a stunning Art Deco blue and white hall with marble pillars and traditional furnishings, then move into a tranquil drawing-room filled with smartly dressed couples enjoying an excellent tea and polite conversation.

What to see:
Bond Street starts near Oxford Street and ends at Piccadilly. It mainly contains shops and boutiques of men's and women's designer wear, but there are also art galleries, antique shops and restaurants.

Health and wealth create beauty.

Fortnum & Mason

181 Piccadilly
Telephone: (0171) 734 8040

Fortnum & Mason seems to be one of the few certainties of London life; it's unchanging, always appears to have been there and has its own special style of service. Situated on the fourth floor is the St James's restaurant. It has the atmosphere of an old-fashioned parlour and serves a jolly good tea.

What to see:

Apsley House, Piccadilly W1. The Duke of Wellington lived in this house after the Napoleonic Wars. It contains some fine paintings, furniture and souvenirs from the Iron Duke, and is open to the public. Please check opening times.

THE TEA:
A set afternoon tea of sandwiches, scones with cream and preserve, then one of those outrageously large cream confections perhaps! A treasure trove of teas includes Royal Blend, Orange Pekoe and iced tea. High tea is also available. Price £10.50.

OPEN:
Monday to Saturday 3.00 to 5.30pm.

GETTING THERE:
Nearest tube Piccadilly Circus. Numerous buses travel to the area. Meter parking.

A man's house is his castle.

Liberty's

Regent Street
Telephone: (0171) 734 1234

Liberty's, founded in 1924, has maintained its delightful, old-fashioned charm up to the present day. It's the sort of store you can browse around in for a good while. You'll see everything from fashion to pottery, from the latest design to the finest of antiques. All the wood used in the building comes from 18th- and 19th-century warships. Tea is served in the fourth floor restaurant, decorated with traditional Liberty prints and colours.

What to see:

Regent Street and the surrounding areas offer an infinite variety of shopping experiences. There are department stores, small shops, designer shops, specialist shops, and many more. Within walking distance are the narrow streets of Soho and several West End theatres.

THE TEA:
There are many tea items as well as set teas on the menu. Look for the Liberty tea: freshly made sandwiches, scones with preserve and cream, special pastries, offered with some fine teas. Price: from £7.95

OPEN:
Monday to Saturday from 3.30pm onwards.

GETTING THERE:
Nearest tube Oxford Circus, many buses travel along Regent Street. Meter parking.

Little and often fills the purse.

Dear Patricia,

<u>Do</u> stop going on about Pebble Mill - nobody ever watches it anyway. <u>I</u> thought you were wonderful ...

The national drink of Ireland is not the "black stout", but the "milky tea". The "cup of tay and itself" were sometimes the only things that made life worth living, as the rain came through the thatch. I was reared on the stuff, but this may not be a recommendation ...

With kind regards.

Yours sincerely,

Terry Wogan.

Maison Bertaux

28 Greek Street
Telephone: (0171) 437 6007

When wandering through the varied streets of Soho, do stop here to admire the cake and pastry display. Maison Bertaux is probably the oldest and best loved teashop that the area has to offer. Established in 1871, there have only been three owners: the Bertaux family; in 1909 the Vignaude family who'd worked for the Bertaux; and in 1988 Michelle who'd worked for the Vignaudes! Take tea upstairs or downstairs; the atmosphere is cheery, bustling and old-fashioned.

What to see:
Take a stroll around Soho to discover a large selection of dress shops, gift shops, designer shops, and a selection of pubs, wine bars and restaurants lining the narrow old streets.

THE TEA:
The selection of pastries, tarts and gateaux is one of the most passionate and irresistible you'll find anywhere! A small choice of teas includes Indian, Rosehip and Mint. Prices are most reasonable.

OPEN:
Monday to Saturday 9.00am to 7.00pm, Sunday 9.30am to 1.00pm and 3.30 to 6.30pm.

GETTING THERE:
Nearest tubes Piccadilly Circus or Leicester Square. Numerous buses travel to the area. Meter parking.

Who is contented enjoys.

Maison Sagne

105 Marylebone High Street
Telephone: (0171) 935 6240

Maison Sagne is an unchanging tea room, amidst a parade of smart shops on the busy High Street. It has maintained its original interior and an excellent standard of baking. As you may have realised, everything is made and baked on the premises.

What to see:
Places to visit in the area include Madame Tussaud's, The Planetarium, Regent's Park and the Wallace Collection.

THE TEA:
A symphony of memorable delights to share – scones, croissants, chocolate, marzipan and cream confections. Teas served are Indian and China. Price: from £4 for a pot of tea and a pastry.

OPEN:
Monday to Friday 9.00am to 5.00pm, Saturday 9.00am to 12.30pm. Closed Sunday.

GETTING THERE:
Nearest tubes Baker Street and Marble Arch, then a walk along Marylebone High Street. Meter parking for cars.

Enough is as good as a feast.

THE TEA:

The restaurant itself is nouveau-Ritz style, a painting here, silk drapes there and gold fringing on comfortable, small armchairs. Afternoon tea, with all the trimmings, is excellent, and if you like the tea set you can buy it on the way out. Price: afternoon tea from £14.50.

OPEN:

Monday to Saturday from 4-5.30pm for tea. Lunch and dinner also served.

GETTING THERE:

Nearest tube Hyde Park Corner. Many buses travel to the area. Only meter parking in the area.

Knowledge finds its price.

The Restaurant at Thomas Goode

19, Audley Street
Telephone: (0171) 409 7242

At first you may feel a little baffled. The sign above the building clearly says Thomas Goode & Co 1876, but the windows are filled with thousands of pieces of glittering crystal and fragile china, not tables, chairs and smiling waiters. The address clearly states 19, Audley Street. Ah! There it is, in the corner, you're home and dry.

What to see:

There are plenty of interesting places to shop, ranging from the bustle of Oxford Street and the elegant stores of Regent Street, to the smart, designer shops of Bond Street and South Molton Street. The Wallace Collection, housed in an elegant 18th-century house, contains a riveting collection of paintings, china and furniture.

THE TEA:

A full traditional tea consists of sandwiches, scones with preserve and cream, a choice of pastries and a selection of teas – Indian, Earl Grey or China. Price: from £15.50

OPEN:

Daily 3.00 to 5.30pm. Booking is essential.

GETTING THERE:

Nearest tube Green Park, several buses pass the entrance. Meter parking for cars.

The Ritz

Piccadilly
Telephone: (0171) 493 8181

Whether your choice is the crowded gaiety of a lively café, or the peace and quiet of a genteel tea room, the Ritz serves tea in the memorable atmosphere of the Palm Court and warrants a visit. The high ceilings, rich ornamentation and fading gilded furniture are all to be admired and treasured.

What to see:

Green Park, created in 1660, is truly green – the only flowers to divert the eye are daffodils in March. Almost every Sunday there is an informal art display on the Piccadilly side. St James's Park was a promenade for the Court.

If one will not, another will.

Still Too Few

300 Westbourne Grove
Telephone: (0171) 727 7752

At first glance 'Still Too Few' at the start of London's lively Portobello market, looks more like an antique emporium than a tea shop. Opening the door however, reveals a distinctly original stop for tea. Every corner of this amazing shop is filled with a fine assortment of antique lights, china, posters, advertisements and odd and enviable food-related collectors items! It's a fascinating place for lingering over tea.

What to see:

From Notting Hill Gate a short walk brings one to the famous and colourful Portobello Road Market (best on Saturdays) where just about anything sold is termed 'Antique'. Genuine bargains are hard to come by but you never know, they are to be found!

THE TEA:
There are always four or five home-made cakes, including a rich chocolate that goes so well with a warming cup of tea. Savoury sandwiches and a cream tea are also on the menu. Prices are reasonable, from £3.50.

OPEN:
Saturdays only! 10.00am to 5.00pm.

GETTING THERE:
Nearest tube Notting Hill Gate. Many buses travel to the area. Parking is possible.

Second thoughts are best.

London WC2
The Crypt, St Martin-in-the-Fields

St Martin's Place
Telephone: (0171) 839 4342

How exquisite is the calm dignity of this church, which dates back to 1726, and how fortunate it is that the crypt has been restored. It was an ancient burial place; among those given a place here were Nell Gwynne and Thomas Chippendale. As you cross the flagstone floor, take a moment and glance down – it makes fascinating reading.

What to see:

Places to visit in the area include Trafalgar Square, The National Gallery, The National Portrait Gallery and the shops and market at Covent Garden.

THE TEA:
Visitors can have tea anytime of the day, choosing from the array of cakes and tea goodies on display, most of which are baked on the premises. Indian, China and a variety of refreshing herb and fruit teas are served. Price: from £3.50.

OPEN:
Monday to Saturday 10.00am to 8.00pm, Sunday 10.00am to 6.00pm.

GETTING THERE:
Nearest tube Charing Cross, many buses travel to Trafalgar Square.

Silence and thinking can no man offend.

The Savoy

The Strand
Telephone: (0171) 836 4343

There are few sensations more enjoyable than entering the revolving doors of the Savoy Hotel, descending the graduated staircase, and arriving at the Thames Foyer for a superb afternoon tea. It is a near-perfect setting; a trompe l'oeil garden surrounds you, complemented by beautiful Art Deco mirrors. Settle down into a comfortable sofa and enjoy the ambience. In a bygone era, many personalities and entertainers performed in cabaret at the Savoy – Chevalier, Coward and Gershwin to name but a few. The style of that era persists to the present day.

What to see:

Covent Garden is a lively and colourful area with many shops, pubs and restaurants. It is the home of the Royal Opera House and some of London's oldest theatres, including the Theatre Royal in Drury Lane.

THE TEA:

A selection of finger sandwiches, warmed, buttered scones, clotted cream, strawberry jam and delicate pastries, served with a choice of teas – China, Indian, Ceylon and herbal. Price: £15.95.

OPEN:

Daily 3.00 to 5.30pm.

GETTING THERE:

Nearest tube Charing Cross, many buses travel to the Strand. Meter parking.

Time tries all things.

The Waldorf Tea Dance

Aldwych
Telephone: (0171) 836 2400

The Waldorf comes alive every weekend with its fabulous tea dances. What could be nicer than to relax in the Palm Court, sip champagne, and tango or waltz as the mood takes you? The Tea Dance is held in the Palm Court every Saturday and Sunday. If you don't wish to participate, just settle down and watch the dancing world glide by.

What to see:

A walk along the Strand will bring you to St Clement Danes church, built by Sir Christopher Wren in 1680. It was badly damaged in the last war, but now restored, it is the RAF church.

THE TEA:

A selection of freshly cut sandwiches and bridge rolls, toasted English muffins, scones with jam and Devon clotted cream and fresh pastries or cream gateaux. Teas served include Earl Grey, Darjeeling, Lapsang Souchong and the Waldorf's special blend. Price: £20.50.

OPEN:

Saturday and Sunday 3.00 to 6.00pm.

GETTING THERE:

Nearest tube Aldwych. Numerous buses travel to the area.

Time lost cannot be recalled.

Peg Woffington Cottage

137 High Street, Teddington
Telephone: (0181) 977 5796

The cottage is famous for its associations with Peg Woffington, a noted 18th-century actress who appeared at Drury Lane and Covent Garden. Open the door and you'll discover a setting of considerable charm: open fireplace, grandfather clock and thirties cinema posters – of Anna Neagle in the role of Old Peg. In Summer take tea in the country garden, filled with roses, and let time stand still.

What to see:
There is an enormous amount to see and do in the area: walks along the river, Hampton Court and its gardens, Richmond, with its river views and 3000 acres of park and much more besides.

THE TEA:
Here you can sample biscuits, crumpets, teacakes and offerings of homely cakes. The set menu of scones, cream and preserves with simmering pots of tea costs £2.50

OPEN:
Saturday and Sunday 3.30 to 6.00pm for tea.

GETTING THERE:
British Rail to Teddington. There's parking for cars.

Time works wonders.

Norfolk
Norfolk Lavender

Caley Mill, Heacham
Telephone: (01485) 570384

As one approaches Caley Mill, the colours and scent of lavender fill the air, it is England's only lavender farm. On a summer afternoon it's a delight to have tea in such an unusual setting.

What to see:
The portrait of the North American Indian princess, Pocahontas, appears on the Heacham village sign. She married John Rolfe of Heacham Hall in 1614, but died in 1617 leaving a young son. From Heacham a road leads to the Wash where there is a beach of sand and shingle at low tide. At Hunstanton the cliffs are naturally striped and are a famous local feature.

THE TEA:
The Miller's Cottage tea room offers scones and home-made cakes served with a small choice of teas. Price: from £2.

OPEN:
Daily 11.00am to 5.00pm. Closed over Christmas. The centre is at its best during the season.

GETTING THERE:
Heacham is on the A149. Caley Mill is close by. Ample parking.

Eat at pleasure drink by measure.

The Old Barn Tearoom

Wroxham Barns, Wroxham
Telephone: (01603) 783762

Close to Wroxham and set in ten acres of parkland is this comfortable, country place. It is a collection of 18th-century barns and buildings that have been reborn as small shops and art and working craft galleries. The sort of place you will want to wander, shop, sit and drink in the scenery, or maybe a classic cup of tea.

What to see:

It is the main centre for cruising the Norfolk Broads, and boats can be hired from several firms. It is also a good place for watching all the messing about that goes on down by the river. Horning and Hoveton are two other boating centres. The Broads are not that accessible to walkers or drivers.

THE TEA:

In the Old Barn, cream tea connoisseurs claim their scones are the best in the area, and the cakes, tarts and shortbread can all be vouched for. Come for breakfast and lunch as well. Price: from £3.50

OPEN:

Daily, all year from 10.00am to 4.30pm. Closed Christmas.

GETTING THERE:

The Barns are signposted off the A1151, north of Wroxham. Own car park.

Love does much, money does everything.

The Owl Tea Rooms

Holt
Telephone: (01263) 713232

A local should be somewhere you can pop into for a cuppa and bump into friends, take children, not have to book a week in advance. Above all, it should offer friendly food in considerate surroundings-The Owl Tea Rooms seems to fit the bill admirably.

What to see:

John Gresham, former Lord Mayor of London founded the renowned Greshams public school here in 1555. From Holt it is easy to explore the north Norfolk coast and of course the Broads. King's Lynn is a few miles in one direction, Norwich a few miles in the other.

THE TEA:

Come in for breakfast, lunch and tea! Specialities of the house include flapjacks, chocolate fudge cake and sticky toffee concoctions. There are set teas and have-what-you-fancy-teas. Something for everyone. Price: from £3.

OPEN:

All year, Monday to Saturday from 9.00am to 5.00pm. Closed Sunday.

GETTING THERE:

Holt is on the A148. Parking in the town.

Fingers were made before forks.

Sharon's Pantry

Little Walsingham
Telephone: (01328) 820686

Sharon's Pantry, half tea room, half bakery represents the good things waiting to be discovered in this part of Norfolk. The decor is simple and rustic, and the clientele is a mix of visitors and well-fed locals, who bring their families to feast on crusty loaves, cream-filled meringues and other equally must-taste goodies.

What to see:
This village of medieval and Georgian houses, set among fields and woodland, is among the most beautiful in England. Until the Reformation, the pilgrimage to the shrine of Our Lady was of great importance and made by kings and commoners alike. In recent years the abbey has been rebuilt and the tradition revived. The myths and legends telling the story of the area are fascinating.

THE TEA:
You'll appreciate good old fashioned pastries, gateaux, breads and baked savouries, and the cream teas will leave you completely satisfied. Stay for breakfast, lunch and tea. Price: from £3.50.

OPEN:
Daily, 8.30 to 8.30 in summer. Winter opening 9.00am to 5.00pm.

GETTING THERE:
Little Walsingham is signposted off the A148 on the B1105. Parking in the village.

Faithfulness is a sister of love.

Whalebone House

Cley-Next-The-Sea
Telephone: (01263) 740336

Whalebone may seem a rum name for a tea room, but, it is surely one of life's little pleasures discovering why favourite places have the names they do! So, for the ever curious, park yourself in a corner, and enjoy an afternoon of comfort.

What to see:
Cley is in the centre of the north Norfolk coast, now officially protected for its beauty and its wildlife. Inland are unspoilt villages, woods and parks. There are stately homes and cathedrals and old fashioned seaside resorts such as Cromer and Blakeney. Sandringham, the Royal Christmas residence, is a big draw, but check opening times.

Man says so! so!
Heaven says no! no!

THE TEA:
There is something invigorating about the choices for tea. On any day, there will be home-made bread and biscuits, and the dresser may be garnished with banana cake, chocolate cake, or shortbread and cherry and almond slices. A variety of light lunches and sandwiches are always available. Price: from £3.

OPEN:
Easter to October, Tuesday to Sunday from 10.30 to 5.30pm. November to Easter, open Wednesday to Sunday only 10.30am to 5.30pm.

GETTING THERE:
Cley is on the A149. Parking in the village.

THE TEA:

This is an informal self-service tea room offering sandwiches, scones, and some good home-made cakes served with pots of tea. Price: from £2.50.

OPEN:

April to end of September: Sunday to Friday 10.00am to 6.00pm. Closed Saturday and October to Easter.

GETTING THERE:

Great Bircham is on the B1153. Nearest main road A148. Own car park.

In the land of hope there is no winter.

Windmill Tea Room

Great Bircham
Telephone: (01485) 578393

The mill still grinds corn and bread is baked for sale in the shop. It is ideal for families as there's plenty to do and see here, with exhibitions, pony rides, sheep, chickens, other farm animals and a well kept garden.

What to see:

King's Lynn merits a visit particularly to see the medieval quarter alongside the river. Strolling along the quays, through alleys and courtyards into the market square is pleasure in itself. In addition there are some fine buildings and cathedral size churches. Royal Sandringham is open at certain times of the year, when the Royal Family are not in residence.

THE TEA:

Teas have always been special with country cakes and light gateaux, but there's a choice of half a dozen or so other dishes, including light bites and healthy food options. Tea choices are offered. Price: from £3.

OPEN:

Monday to Saturday from 9.00am to 5.00pm. Closed Sunday.

GETTING THERE:

Earls Barton is east of Northampton on the A45. Nearest motorway M1. Parking in the village.

Every Jack has his Jill.

Northamptonshire
Apothocoffee Shop

Earls Barton
Telephone: (01604) 810289

Walking through Earls Barton, with its village square and Norman church, is a stroll back in time. Old houses are still used as family homes and one of the shops is the oldest surviving business in the village. Now called the Apothocoffee Shop, it offers three things-tablets, treasures and teas.

What to see:

The county is well known for its high-spired churches and for its unusual historical associations: it has two 'Eleanor Crosses' erected in the 13th century by Edward I wherever his wife's coffin rested on its journey to burial in Westminster Abbey. Fotheringhay is where Mary Queen of Scots was executed though only a fragment of the castle now remains.

Holdenby House

Holdenby, Northampton
Telephone: (01604) 770074

In Elizabethan times Holdenby was the largest house in the country. Today only a fraction of the original remains, but the grounds and gardens have been restored in the original style. The appealing Victorian Tea Room offers refreshment and is open on Sundays and Bank Holiday Mondays during the season.

What to see:
Today the house provides the backdrop to a family day out with beautiful gardens, animal and falconry centres. To commemorate the Battle of Naseby the Sealed Knot Society will re-enact it at Holdenby in June. This part of the county has agreeable countryside, easily reached from the M1. A special feature is water-rivers, canals, lakes and reservoirs dotted everywhere.

THE TEA:
Visitors can sample a small but tasty range of home-made cakes, scones with cream and jam served with pots of tea or coffee. Price: from £2.50

OPEN:
The season is from April to the end of September. The gardens are open weekdays and Sundays. Closed Saturdays. The house is open 3 Bank Holiday Mondays only. Please phone to check.

GETTING THERE:
Holdenby is signposted off the A50, A428 roads. Nearest motorway M1. Own car park.

A little too late, much too late.

Jessica's Tea Shop

At Weekley Post Office
Telephone: (01536) 82312

Roses round the door, cottage garden, small-paned windows, fireplaces, nooks and crannies are the first things that strike the visitor. Jessica's, on the way into the village, is a post office-cum-tea-room and as beguiling a place as you could ever hope to chance upon.

What to see:
Stately Homes such as Althorp, Rockingham Castle and Burghley House are worth a visit. Oundle is an attractive town of honey coloured stone, the famous school buildings are like an Oxford college. At Kettering, discover Wicksteed Park, an amusement park created in the 1930s and ideal for a family outing.

Speech is silver, silence is golden.

THE TEA:
High marks for the interesting and unmissable choices of cakes, including some sugar free and wholemeal varieties. The fine scones and teabreads are accompanied by a splendid list of teas.
Price: from £3.

OPEN:
Monday to Saturday from 9.00am to 5.00pm. Sunday from 11-5.00pm. Closed Wednesday.

GETTING THERE:
Weekley is north of Kettering on the A43. Nearest motorway M1. Parking in the village.

FRANKIE VAUGHAN O.B.E., D.L.

Dear Patricia Rose,

Mr. and Mrs. Vaughan are tea addicts.   They

start their morning with two cups and when

they come downstairs they make another cup.

of tea.

I hope this is helpful to you.

Yours sincerely,

Barbara Langstone (Mrs)
Personal Secretary to
Frankie Vaughan

Teapots

High Street, Olney
Telephone, Bookshop, (01234) 712176

The tea room is small and low-ceilinged, with pale walls, a glowing fire and a long pine counter busily filled with vintage cakes and the finest of sponges. Even the name 'Teapots' is enticing; once you are there, the visit, however brief, will be tickety-boo, the ladies will make sure of that. The next-door shop offers a quality selection of books.

What to see:
The Olney Hymns were written here by John Cowper (1731-1800) and another famous resident was John Newton, the former slave trader who saw the error of his ways and became pastor of Olney. There is a small museum dedicated to both of them. It is a mellow village to wander through with attractive, small shops, pubs and a church.

THE TEA:
Needless to say, all the baking is fresh and homespun and sandwiches and snacks are all made to order. The tea list also offers several choices. Price: from £3.

OPEN:
Monday to Saturday from 10.00am to 5.00pm. Sunday from 2-5.00pm.

GETTING THERE:
Olney is on the A509 road. Nearest motorway M1. Limited parking in the village.

Little things are pretty.

Northumberland
Belsay Hall

Belsay
Telephone: (01661) 881636

Belsay Hall is one of the most important neo-classical houses in Britain completed in 1815, together with an intact 14th-century tower house and a ruined 17th-century mansion house. A new tea room has been opened within the Old Kitchens and is a most appealing stop for tea.

What to see:
At Belsay the thirty acre gardens are a delight and there are occasional guided tours detailing the varied fauna and flora. Please check for more details. The village of Belsay was re-modelled during the 19th century and the buildings have an Italianate appearance.

This morning knows not this evenings happenings.

THE TEA:
A selection of sandwiches, scones, cakes and pastries is available along with light meals and snacks. A limited range of teas is available. Price: from £3.

OPEN:
Monday to Sunday 10.30am to 5.00pm during the season. October weekends only then closed. Please check opening times.

GETTING THERE:
Belsay in north-west of Newcastle on the A696. Nearest motorway A1(M). Own car park.

The Chantry Tea Rooms

Chantry Place, Morpeth
Telephone: (01670) 514414

It is always a pleasure to find a place like The Chantry. It has an atmosphere of genuine hospitality. Once you've settled in and tickled your tastebuds, look round at the original paintings and photos on the walls, many of which are for sale.

What to see:

Northumberland is a county of great estates, and not far from Morpeth, is one of the largest, Wallington Hall. Belsay and Cragside are also easily reached. Further away is the Northumbrian coast, with miles of deserted beaches, ruined castles and Farne Island. Boat trips are organised to the islands to watch seals and puffins.

THE TEA:

A variety of snacks, sandwiches, puddings and cakes are served, and all are very tasty. The favourite, though, has to be the cream tea, with tender scones and home-made jams. Good tea choices. Price: from £3.

OPEN:

Monday to Saturday from 10.00am to 5.00pm. All year round. Closed Sunday.

GETTING THERE:

Morpeth is on the A1(M). Parking in the town.

Fair and softly goes far.

The Tea Cosy Tea Rooms

Northumberland Street, Alnmouth
Telephone: (01665) 830393

Just seeing the name 'Tea Cosy' makes you smile. Push open the door, the place is creamy and comforting. The walls are thick, old stone. The fireplace glows. The laden dresser sets the taste buds buzzing. Ah yes, this will do nicely, thank you.

What to see:

Nearby is the seat of the Duke of Northumberland, who lives in Alnwick castle. There are walks to follow, ruins to discover and a coastline dotted with many a castle. Alnmouth is an attractive yachting resort and has one of England's oldest golf courses. During the season there are frequent boat trips to Farne and Holy Islands.

THE TEA:

One can't go wrong with a tea of scones or slabs of rich chocolate cake. Save room for a 'Singin Hinny' or some call-again cake, and you will, served with pots of tea, with tea cosies, of course. Price: from £3.

OPEN:

Daily in summer 9.00am to 6.00pm. Winter 10.00am to 5.00pm. Friday, Saturday 6-9.30pm.

GETTING THERE:

Alnmouth is on the A1068, B13339 roads. Parking in the town

That which suffices is not little.

The Copper Kettle

21 Front Street, Bamburgh
Telephone: (01668) 214315

After touring Bamburgh Castle, linger over a slice of cake and a pot of tea at this charming welcoming old-fashioned tea room with its lovely cottage garden.

What to see:
The unspoilt village of Bamburgh is dominated by the impressive Norman castle. Grace Darling, the lighthouse keeper's daughter who with her father rescued survivors from a wrecked steamer, is buried in the graveyard of the fine 13th-century church. The cable they used and other souvenirs of the heroic rescue are in the Grace Darling museum.

THE TEA:
The display counter is filled with a selection of pastries, home-made scones, chocolate cakes, shortbread and fruit slices – all irresistible. There is a good choice of Indian, China and herbal teas. Price: from £2.50.

OPEN:
March to November: daily 10.30am to 5.30pm. Closed early November to early March.

GETTING THERE:
Bamburgh is on the B1340, B1341 and B1342 roads. Nearest main road A1. Parking in the village.

I am willing to taste any drink once.
– James Cabell

The White Monk Tea Room

The Square, Blanchland, near Consett
Telephone: (01434675) 276

Just a stone's throw from the River Derwent is one of the nicest village tea rooms in the region. The atmosphere is friendly and welcoming and visitors are quickly made to feel at home. Good home-baking and value for money make return visits inevitable.

What to see:
There can be few English villages more beautiful than Blanchland, it is surrounded by moorland and is almost hidden, so that you seem to stumble upon it as if by accident. The village was created from mellow stones taken from the ruins of the medieval abbey. The 13th-century abbey church chancel was rebuilt as the parish church.

If the beginning is good, the end must be perfect.

THE TEA:
Go with a good appetite for freshly made sandwiches, brown bread with home-made jams plus fruity scones and slices of delicious cake. All served with steaming pots of tea. Prices are very reasonable, from £2.50.

OPEN:
Daily 2.00 to 5.00pm. Closed October to Easter.

GETTING THERE:
Blanchland is on the B6306. Nearest motorway A1(M). Village car park.

THE TEA:
In a relaxing, comfortable atmosphere hymn your way through some unpretentious home-made cakes and scones with several choices of tea. Price: from £3.

OPEN:
Daily from 10.00am to 5 00pm. All year round.

GETTING THERE:
Nottingham is on the A60, A52 and A602 roads. Nearest motorway M1. Car parks in the town centre.

It is good to be neither too high nor too low.

The Lace Hall

High Pavement, Nottingham
Telephone: (0115) 9484 221

The relationship between architecture and food is a fascinating one. Does, where you eat have an effect on how much you enjoy what you eat? If unusual places for tea interest youthen visit the Lace Hall. Housed in a former chapel, with beautiful stained glass windows, you'll discover the story of Nottingham lace, two shops and a corner especially carved out for tea.

What to see:
Nottinghamshire is one of those counties often ignored by tourists-which means that it is less crowded for those who appreciate its many attractions. Among them you'll discover: farm parks, Robin Hood shows, canal trips, exhibitions and the National Mining Museum. Newark is another town rich in history and well worth a visit.

THE TEA:
Afterwards, what better than a Longdale high tea with home-made scones and cakes accompanied by a choice of Earl Grey, Indian and herbal tea blends. Snacks and light meals also available. Price: from £3.50.

OPEN:
Monday to Sunday 10.00am to 10.00pm.

GETTING THERE:
Ravenshead is on the A60 road. Nearest motorway M1. Own car park.

Longdale Rural Craft Centre

Longdale Lane, Ravenshead
Telephone: (01623) 794858

This is the headquarters of the Nottinghamshire Craftsmen's Guild. Here, in a pleasant atmosphere you'll want to spend time browsing amid the workshops offering stained glass, wood carving, or jewellery or visiting the small village museum.

What to see:
Nottinghamshire is a county with much to offer in the way of family attractions. You will discover farm parks, Robin Hood shows, adventure and theme parks, canal trips and the National Mining Museum. Newark, with its large market square and castle ruins is the town where King John died in 1216.

Diligence makes an expert workman.

The Abbey Tearooms

Dorchester-on-Thames
Telephone: (01865) 340044

There are some tea rooms which immediately have a good feel about them and somehow you are sure you are in the right place –the Abbey is one such place. A group of inspired ladies hase turned the Old Guest House into a most convivial and entertaining place for tea. Two tables, one oblong, one round, to encourage friendly chatter and maybe a friendship or two are already laid for tea; so find a seat and look forward to an enjoyable afternoon.

What to see:
The Abbey Church holds a wealth of treasures and the Guest House is now a museum. A walk along the main street is full of interest.

THE TEA:
The well-presented tables are full of plump scones, crisp shortbread and an ever changing assortment of cakes. Price: from £3.

OPEN:
Wednesday, Thursday, Saturday, Sunday and Bank Holidays from the Saturday before Easter until the end of September: 3.00pm until the food runs out.

GETTING THERE:
Dorchester-on-Thames is well signposted on the A423. Car parking in the village.

Content is more than a Kingdom.

Andrews Hotel

High Street, Burford
Telephone: (0199382) 3151

Burford is one of the most interesting Cotswold towns with cobbled byways, small inns and plenty of craft and antique shops. Andrews Hotel lies along the picturesque main street. This lovely old house of warm Cotswold stone is beautifully furnished with antiques, interesting paintings and comfortable armchairs grouped around the old fireplaces. In the country garden tea is served on summer afternoons.

What to see:
Within easy reach of Burford there are a great many other towns and villages of great charm. A wildlife park and bird gardens are a short drive away offering attractions for the family.

Virtue is found in the middle.

THE TEA:
The table is laden with warmed scones, clotted cream and delicious preserve, so please help yourself. There are always muffins and crumpets on the menu as well as some well chosen leaf teas. Price for the set tea is around £5 rising to £8.

OPEN:
Daily, tea is served from 3.00 to 5.00pm.

GETTING THERE:
Burford is east of Oxford on the A40. Parking is permitted in the village.

Annie's Tea Rooms

79 High Street, Wallingford
Telephone: (01491) 836308

Annie's is a traditional tea room close to the centre of Wallingford, where all the baking is done on the premises. Inside, pictures line the walls of the pink painted room and the atmosphere is informal. Home-made food at its best, at affordable prices makes Annie's an ideal place to bring the whole family.

What to see:
Wallingford is a busy market town with a bustling atmosphere situated on the west bank of the picturesque River Thames spanned by a 12th-century bridge. In addition, the town boasts the attractive Lamb Arcade of period shops, a town hall and the Corn Exchange theatre, together with its own private railway.

THE TEA:
The set teas, including a scrumptious cream tea with delicious home-made jam, and a selection of old fashioned classic cakes are very popular. A good range of teas is offered. Price: from £3.

OPEN:
Monday to Saturday 10.00am to 5.00pm. Closed Wednesday, Sunday and Bank Holidays. Open for Teas on Sundays 2.30 to 5.30pm July to September.

GETTING THERE:
Wallingford is south-east of Oxford on the A329. The town's car parks are pay and display.

There was never enough where nothing was left.

Bridgecombe Farm

Uffington, near Faringdon
Telephone: (0367) 820667

Up the hill beyond the village of Uffington, past the prehistoric White Horse and Waylands Smithy, and tucked away between the folds of the vale is Bridgecombe Farm – home to three generations of the same family! You might easily pass by without a second glance were it not for the sign – a large white teapot! Tea is served in a restored stable, the old fireplace and white painted beams give the place a homely air. On sunny afternoons guests can take tea in the farm garden.

What to see:
In the surrounding Vale of the White Horse there are plenty of good canalside walks. The village of Uffington has memories of Tom Brown (Tom Brown's Schooldays), and the old Ridgeway Path runs here.

THE TEA:
There are always choices of cakes and pastries as well as a set cream tea. Price: from £3.

OPEN:
February to October: Weekends and Bank Holidays only, 3.00 to 5.30pm, Sunday until 6.30pm. November open Sunday only.

GETTING THERE:
Bridgecombe Farm is situated on the B4507 Wantage to Swindon Road. Parking at the farm.

Soon enough if well enough.

Miss Marple Tea Shoppe

29 Broad Street, Abingdon
Telephone: (0235) 555630

In a listed Georgian house in the centre of Abingdon, this is a friendly unpretentious little tea room with half-a-dozen tables and a welcoming atmosphere.

What to see:
Abingdon is one of the oldest towns in the area, and lies near the River Thames, so there are some fine riverside walks. The almshouses and remains of the once powerful abbey church are of interest, as is the 17th-century 'County Hall' now a museum. The old gaol built in 1805, is now an arts and leisure centre.

THE TEA:
The menu is very simple, cakes and scones are all home-made, and the cream tea is always a favourite. A choice of teas, Darjeeling, Earl Grey and lemon, are available. Price: from £2.

OPEN:
Monday to Saturday 9.30am to 5.00pm. Closed Sunday.

GETTING THERE:
Abingdon is on the A415. Nearest motorway M40. Limited street parking and public car park.

Bear with evil and expect good.

Rosie Lee's

High Street, Oxford
Telephone: (01865) 244429

If you enjoy cakes and tea as much as a gossipy atmosphere, but don't want to be stitched up, you would do well to eat at Rosie Lee's, a pillar of Oxford student life, made more picturesque by staff dressed in black and white and graduate patrons, clad in scarves and laden with books.

What to see:
Outside Oxford and away from Blenheim, the appeal of the county lies in the small towns and villages, most of which are relatively unspoilt and perfect for a potter. The countryside is very varied and driving around is pleasant, particularly off the main roads. Another way of seeing the county is by boat on the Thames.

Question for question is all fair.

THE TEA:
Munch happily on a cream tea of scones and jam or refresh yourself with sandwiches, savouries and a selection of cakes-served all day. Price: from £3.50.

OPEN:
Daily from 9.00am to 6.30pm. Weekends to 7.30pm.

GETTING THERE:
Oxford is on the A40 A44 A423 roads. Nearest motorway M40. Pay for parking in the city centre.

The Randolph Hotel

Beaumont Street, Oxford
Telephone: (01865) 247481

Oxford's premier Victorian hotel retains much of the grandeur of a bygone age. Tea is served in the elegant, high-ceilinged drawing room to the gentle strains of 'golden oldies'.

What to see:

Even the most cursory visit to Oxford should include visits to Christ Church (with Oxford Cathedral), Magdalen, Merton, Queen's and New College as well as the Ashmolean Museum and the Sheldonian Theatre. Some curious customs have survived including the annual beating of the city's bounds.

Love and scandal are the best sweeteners of tea.
– Henry Fielding

THE TEA:
Crisp linen and pretty china enhance the traditional teatime choice of generously filled sandwiches followed by scones, preserve and cream, cakes and pastries. Assam, Earl Grey and Darjeeling are three of the tea choices. Price: a traditional tea from £10.

OPEN:
Daily 3.00 to 5.30pm.

GETTING THERE:
Oxford is on the A34, A40, A420 and A423 roads. Nearest motorway M40. There is a park and ride system in operation. Pay and display parking in the city centre.

Shropshire

Acorn

26 Sandford Avenue, Church Stretton
Telephone: (01694) 722495

The ivy covered chalk board is how to find this charming retreat tucked away on the first floor of an old house. Seek it out. It is instantly appealing and seems to have a glowing patina from much use. If the weather is good stroll outside and enjoy tea in the garden.

What to see:

Apart from the scenery of one of England's most peaceful counties, an interesting town to visit is Shrewsbury. There are twisted little lanes to explore, a castle, a pillared market hall and plenty of black-and-white houses.

Believe well and have well.

THE TEA:
This is a place to find good-value wholefood throughout the day. Hot snacks, soups, home-made puddings and cakes go well with a selection of 20 or more teas. Be full, be happy. Price: from £3.50.

OPEN:
Monday to Sunday from 10.00am to 5.30ish. Closed Tuesdays, also November and February for 2 weeks.

GETTING THERE:
Church Stretton is signposted off the A49. Parking in the town.

Clun Bridge Tea Rooms

Clun
Telephone: (01588) 640634

Close your eyes and return to the days when travelling around England seemed to revolve around finding places like the Bridge Tea Rooms on every street corner. It soothes, settles and lives in the memory. The kindly warmth of the place taking its tone from the way it is run, and quite possibly the fire glowing in the old kitchen range.

What to see:

Close to the town are the ruins of a moated Norman castle-once a stronghold in the Marches. A tiny stone bridge carries you over the River Clun, and then on to Clun forest, no trees, but mile upon mile of gently rounded hills that really are knee deep in sheep.

THE TEA:

A variety of snacks and sandwiches are served, but save room for one, or more, of the home-made cakes and scones, Wolf it all down with a good pot of tea. Price: from £3.

OPEN:

Daily from 10.30am to 5.30pm. Closed end of October to Easter.

GETTING THERE:

Clun is on the A488 and B4368 roads. Parking in the town.

Likeness causes liking.

De Grey's

Broad Street, Ludlow
Telephone: (01584) 872764

The general placing is good, just far enough from the hustle and bustle of historic, busy Ludlow, particularly on market days. The 16th-century house has character as well, with old, uneven floors, leaded windows and waitresses traditionally attired-it isn't grand, but it is caring and welcoming.

What to see:

This part of the country is noted for its peace and tranquillity. There are many walking and bird watching opportunities across the Shropshire hills. Ludlow still preserves its priceless half timbered buildings and the crooked alleys that just appeared instead of being planned. It's market square is one of the finest in England and the castle dominates the area for miles around.

THE TEA:

The essence of the menu is consistency. Traditional lunches are followed by Welsh rarebits, assorted pastries, scones and cakes, all of which are baked on the premises. Price from £3.

OPEN:

Monday to Thursday from 9.00am to 5.00pm.(5.30pm) Friday and Saturday.

GETTING THERE:

Ludlow is on the A49. Nearest motorway M5. Parking in the town car parks.

Make do and have do.

115

Dear Patricia

Thank you for your letter, no I'm not a great tea drinker, only when I really fancy a cup. My favourite drink is Whittards Hazelnut Coffee, however I am a great fan of teahouses & tea rooms, a delicous cream teas

May I take this opportunity in wishing you luck with your book.

With love

Lorraine Chase x

Hoo Farm Country Park

Preston On The Weald Moors, Telford
Telephone: (01952) 677917

Animals are everywhere in Shropshire, and a visit to Hoo Farm is no exception. On most weekends though, something a little more unusual is afoot, visitors can try their hand at sheep racing. Rituals such as studying form and exciting commentary are properly observed. How could anyone resist a flutter on Larry the Lamb?

What to see:
On the farm are interesting breeds of cattle, sheep and pigs as well as ostriches, llamas and pheasants, all contributing to a pleasant family day out. Other places of interest in Shropshire are the Georgian town of Ellesmere and its surrounding lakes, the little market town of Wem, and Hodnet, with some fine black-and-white houses.

THE TEA:
Whether or not racing is for you-eating probably is. Farmhouse and cream teas, light snacks, various cakes and home-made ice creams won't leave you down on the day. With these go a good list of hot and cold drinks. Price: from £3.50.

OPEN:
Wednesday to Sunday in summer from 11.00am to 6.00pm. Winter 10.00am to 5.00pm. 25 March to 24 December.

GETTING THERE:
Preston on the Weald Moors is signposted off the A442 A518 roads. Nearest motorway M54. Farm car-park.

The hawk kissed the hen- up to the last feather.

The Malthouse

High Street, Much Wenlock
Telephone: (01952) 728419

Every once in a while it is a pleasure to slip away for a day in search of what England has to offer the unsuspecting visitor. Such an impulse might take you to the serene little town of Much Wenlock, and in to the Malthouse. Whether your taste runs to spotting an antique bargain or settling down to a satisfying tea, you can find them both here.

What to see:
The ruins of the 12th- and 13th-century priory dominate the attractions in the town of Much Wenlock. The county owes its appeal to its distinctive countryside, with several hills of decided character, notably the Long Mynd, offering spectacular views. In between the hills are woods, streams and farming valleys.

THE TEA:
Special afternoon teas here are a local treasure, but a variety of hot snacks and light lunches are generous both in proportion and flavour. Price: from £2.50.

OPEN:
Monday to Saturday from 10.00am to 5.30pm. From 11 on Sundays. Closed Tuesdays in winter.

GETTING THERE:
Much Wenlock is on the A458 road. Nearest motorway M54. Parking in the town.

Every picture tells a story.

Boscobel House

Boscobel
Telephone: (01902) 850244

This timber-framed hunting lodge built at the beginning of the 17th century, and attractively set among later farm buildings is best known for its link with Charles II, who hid in the lodge and a nearby oak tree after the battle of Worcester in 1651.

What to see:

The church at Tong, founded by Elizabeth de Pembruge in the 14th century, has a remarkable collection of tombs and monuments and is one of the wonders of the county. Also in the area are Weston Park, home of the Earls of Bradford, and Chillington Hall standing in one thousand acres of parkland.

Poppy's & The Stables

8 Milk Street, Shrewsbury
Telephone: (01743) 232307

These fascinating premises, dating back to the 18th century, were actually where the fire engine horses were stabled in days gone by. On sunny days the courtyard makes a good setting for outdoor tea.

What to see:

Perched on top of a hill, encircled by a loop of the River Severn, Shrewsbury is rich in history. Discover the castle, the main square, historic houses and twisting lanes with names like Dogpole, and Shoplatch. Shrewsbury has several museums and the one at Clive House, College Hill – the 18th-century home of Clive of India – is especially interesting.

As sound as a bell.

THE TEA:

Here, visitors enjoy a good cup of tea either Indian, Earl Grey or herbal accompanied by sandwiches and a selection of home-made scones and cakes. Price: from £3.50.

OPEN:

Easter to September: Tuesday to Sunday 11.00am to 5.00pm. Sunday only in winter. Closed all of January. House open all year. Please check opening times.

GETTING THERE:

Boscobel House is eight miles north-west of Wolverhampton between the A41 and A5. Nearest motorway M54. Own car park.

Great hopes make great men.

THE TEA:

Delicious scones like cherry or date and walnut make a splendid tea, while other treats include flapjacks, teacakes and pastries. There are eight to ten choices of tea including fruit and herbal. Price: from £3.

OPEN:

Monday to Saturday 9.45am to 4.30pm. Closed Sunday.

GETTING THERE:

Shrewsbury is on the A5, A49 and A458 roads. Nearest motorway M54. Public car parks.

Rococo Rooms, Williams & Williams

High Street, Bridgnorth
Telephone: (01746) 767878

The aromas of home cooking are enough to send you up the stairs to the first floor. There you'll find warmth and intimacy. Domed ceilings, subdued lighting, walls covered with pink-and-white paper, and tables covered with fine china give the Rococo Rooms a glowing, elegant ambience. The effect is very much 'in the pink'.

What to see:
The half timbered town hall divides High Street, with the north gate at one end, and the Georgian houses of East Castle Street at the other, which leads to the church of St. Mary Magdalene, built by Telford in 1794. However the charm of Bridgnorth lies in the medieval atmosphere that pervades its streets of black-and-white houses.

THE TEA:
Mull over a menu offering light snacks, tea breads and assorted cakes and pastries, in fact all your favourite things on a plate, along with a good choice of teas. Price: from £3.

OPEN:
Monday to Saturday from 9.30am to 4.30pm. Closed Sunday.

GETTING THERE:
Bridgnorth is on the A458 A442 roads. Nearest motorways M54 M44. Parking in the town.

Little and often fills the purse.

Six Ashes Tea Room

Six Ashes
Telephone: (01384) 221216

Visitors appreciate the comfort, cosiness and hospitality of this friendly tea room in the little known village of Six Ashes. It is one of those 'tea joys' tucked away hither and thither that one stumbles upon, quite by chance, travelling around the counties of England.

What to see:
Bridgnorth is another of Shropshire's riverside fortified towns and well worth a visit. North of here is the Ironbridge Gorge Museum. Here is the world's first iron bridge. Opened in 1770 it still spans the River Severn. The museum tells the story of the industrial revolution.

THE TEA:
All the cooking and baking is done using good quality ingredients and free range eggs. Expect feathery light scones, creamy cakes and crumbly moist fruit ones. The well spread tea list offers Indian, China, fruit and herbal. Price from £4.

OPEN:
Wednesday to Sunday, summer only, from 10.00am to 5.00pm. Wednesday and Thursday 11.00am to 4.30pm in winter.

GETTING THERE:
Six Ashes is on the A458 road, south of Bridgnorth. Car park near by.

Leave off with an appetite.

119

THE TEA:

The highlight is a full afternoon tea of sandwiches, scones and cakes, but a tea can be put together to suit individual desires. Please book in advance for a special.
Price: from £6.

OPEN:

Everyday from 3.30-5.30pm for tea.

GETTING THERE:

Taunton is on the A38 A358 roads. Nearest motorway M5. Large car park in the front of the hotel.

—◇—

Cold pudding will settle your love.

—◇—

Castle Hotel

Castle Green, Taunton
Telephone: (01823) 272671

The Castle really was a castle, though today the stonework is so festooned by a magnificent wisteria you might not realise. The welcome and service given to residents and non-residents alike is outstanding. Afternoon tea can be taken in the warmth of the Rose Room decorated with paintings, tapestries and floral displays.

What to see:
The River Tone wends its way through Taunton, not a beautiful town, and there are several riverside walks. The historic heart of the town lies around the castle remains which houses a county museum. To the south, the Blackdown hills almost mark the county borders, their length dominated by the town of Wellington's monument to the Iron Duke.

—◇—

THE TEA:

The daily changing selection of home-made scones, biscuits, cakes and gateaux makes a tempting display. There is a choice of tea blends. Price: from £2.50.

OPEN:

Monday to Friday 9.00am to 5.30pm. Closed Saturday afternoon, Sunday and Bank Holidays.

GETTING THERE:

Williton is on the A39 and A358 roads. Nearest motorway M5. Village car park.

—◇—

Eat enough it will make you wise.

—◇—

Blackmore's Bookshop Tea Room

6 High Street, Williton
Telephone: (01984) 632227

After browsing among the well stocked shelves at the Blackmore's bookshop, make your way through to the cosy tea room, just three or four tables, for some tempting light refreshment and a pot of tea. On warm days the garden is a delight. The barn stocks crafts and antiques

What to see:
The village of Williton lies close to the Quantock Hills, an area of natural outstanding beauty. There are magnificent walks with glorious views, and several scenic routes primarily for the motorist. Minehead is a seaside resort with a picturesque quay and harbour; steamers connect with the Bristol Channel ports.

The Cloister Restaurant

Wells Cathedral, Wells
Telephone: (01749) 676543

Situated in the west cloister of this magnificent cathedral, The Cloister Restaurant with its fan vaulted ceiling makes an unusual and tranquil setting for afternoon tea.

What to see:
Wells is a quiet market town at the foot of the Mendip Hills, and makes a good centre for touring. The cathedral dominates the town and is one of the oldest and finest in Somerset. The moated Bishop's Palace, is still used by the bishop and is occasionally open to the public. The swans in the moat ring a bell near the drawbridge to demand bread when they are ready for lunch.

THE TEA:
Whether your taste is for creamy cakes and sponges, or for more 'healthy' home-baking, there is plenty to choose from. Several tea varieties include, Indian, Ceylon and herbal. Price: from £2.25

OPEN:
Monday to Saturday 10.00am to 5.00pm, Sunday 2.00 to 5.00pm. Closed over Christmas.

GETTING THERE:
Wells is on the A39 and A371 roads. Nearest motorway M5. Parking in the town.

Knowledge is the action of the soul.

Lowerbourne House

High Street, Porlock
Telephone: (01643) 862948

Porlock Hill is of such spectacular incline that your car either plummets downwards as if on a big dipper or else crawls up it like a tipsy snail. But it's worth it just to get to Lowerbourne House. Decor treads a line between vintage Victorian and period pine and the staff tread a line between being helpful and becoming a member of the family.

What to see:
Be warned Porlock does get very crowded in the summer season. Two miles west is Porlock Weir, a sturdy village of thatched, colour-washed houses clustered around a harbour. The local inn was a notorious smugglers haunt and the church is one of the smallest in England. The area offers bracing cliff top and country walks.

THE TEA:
The kitchen offers wholesome snacks, tip-top baking and good choices of tea. Everyone agrees that the soft moorland water enhances the taste of the brew. Price: from £3.

OPEN:
Monday to Saturday 10.00am to 5.30pm. Sunday from 11.00am March to December. Closed January and February.

GETTING THERE:
Porlock is on the A38 road. Nearest motorway M5. Parking in the village.

Time will tell.

THE TEA:
From 2.30pm onwards afternoon teas are served, with a good selection of tempting home baking. There are scones, flapjacks, sponges and fruit cakes. There is a choice of tea blends. Price: from £3.

OPEN:
Easter to December: Monday to Sunday 12.30 to 5.30pm. Closed Tuesday and December to Easter. The house is open Easter to October. Please check opening times.

GETTING THERE:
Montacute is on the A3088 (A37 A303) roads. Nearest Motorway M5. Own car park.

THE TEA:
There is an excellent choice of teas served with flapjacks, fruit loaves, wholemeal scones and an array of delicious home-baked cakes. Price: from £2.50.

OPEN:
Tuesday to Saturday 9.30am to 5.00pm. Closed Sunday and Monday.

GETTING THERE:
Castle Cary is off the A359 and A371 roads. Nearest motorway M5. Street parking and town car parks.

Montacute House

Montacute
Telephone: (0935) 824575

Montacute House was built between 1588 – 1601 for Sir Edward Phelips and is one of the finest examples of a Tudor mansion in existence. In the old laundry of this splendid house with its magnificent gardens is the popular tea room.
What to see:
The contents of the house includes panelling, plasterwork, tapestries and furniture. The Long Gallery contains portraits on loan from the National Portrait Gallery. The formal gardens with big lawns and yew trees are immaculately kept.

Speak fitly, or be silent wisely.

Old Bakehouse

Castle Cary
Telephone: (01963) 350067

The old walls, small windows, wooden tables and chairs all make for cosy surroundings at the Old Bakehouse. The menu is dedicated to wholesome home-baking and on warm days afternoon tea is most enjoyable in the courtyard garden. The atmosphere is convivial and welcoming.
What to see:
The Norman castle has long since gone, but the town is still steeped in history. The old town centre has a duckpond and an unusual round 18th-century lock-up, just seven feet in diameter. The streets are lined with rows of pleasant old shops and houses. The church is worth a visit, only the 15th-century pulpit escaped destruction by Cromwell's Roundheads.

Measure is treasure.

Periwinkle Cottage

Selworthy Green
Telephone: (01643) 862769

A periwinkle and rose garden, looking onto the village green and across to Exmoor, provides a pleasing welcome to this thatched cottage. Step inside, and enter a charming and homely tea room, with a feast of home-baking to match.

What to see:
All the villages in the Vale of Porlock are picturesque, but Selworthy is perhaps the most well known. It has the best views, and nearly all the cottages are old and thatched. The church has a 14th-century tower and is most eye catching being white, externally. The walk to Selworthy Beacon is a treat and well worth doing!

All things require skill but an appetite.

Settle

15 Cheap Street, Frome
Telephone: (013734) 65975

This cheery, traditional tea shop stands in the heart of an old paved street with a little stream running down the middle. Everything on the menu is home-made and the range of cakes and pastries is incredibly diverse, the atmosphere is busy, bustling and cheerful.
Price: from £3.

What to see:
This is a busy, lively market town on the River Frome, with steep medieval streets. The parish church dates from the 12th century and was extensively restored in Victorian times, nearby is the local history museum. In 1685 Monmouth and his army spent a night here, as a consequence twelve men were later hanged in the Market Place by the King's order.

THE TEA:
Start with freshly baked scones and clotted cream, before feasting on a variety of sponges, fruit and nut tarts and chocolate fudge cakes. Tea choices include Darjeeling, Earl Grey and several more. Price: from £2.

OPEN:
March to October: Tuesday to Sunday 10.00am to 5.00pm. Closed Monday, except Bank Holidays.

GETTING THERE:
Selworthy Green is off the A39 Porlock road. Nearest motorway M5. Parking in the village.

THE TEA:
There are meringues, scones, cheese muffins, chocolate cakes and Frome bobbins – fruit soaked in cider and wrapped in pastry. There is a range of fine teas.

OPEN:
Monday to Saturday 9.00am to 5.00pm. Sunday and Bank Holidays 2.30 to 6.30pm. Closed Thursday from 2.00pm and Sundays October to April.

GETTING THERE:
Frome is on the A359 and A362 roads. Nearest motorway M4. Limited street parking.

Hours of pleasure are short.

DONALD SINDEN, C.B.E., F.R.S.A.

Dear Mr Cress,

      How right you are! — I am a Tea-man. My day begins with 2 cups of Fortnums Royal Blend (Never tea bags!) and again in the afternoon* (I cannot stand China tea) My wife and I prefer our tea unbelievably weak — one teaspoonful in a six-cup pot and we drink it without milk or sugar or lemon. There are still a number of places who provide wonderful cream teas and we search them out — in London, the Savoy, Ritz and Waldorf. Last year in Sheffield I requested "Two Cream Teas, please". A mystified young waiter asked me to repeat the order and then returned with a pot of tea and a jug of cream!

       Best wishes

          Donald Sinden

* also late at night

Tea Shoppe

High Street, Dunster
Telephone: (01643) 821304

This charming 15th-century cottage has retained some fine original features further enhanced, with a display counter said to have come from Dunster Castle, and polished wooden tables and chairs. Service is friendly and the atmosphere homely.
What to see:
There is much to see in Dunster. Of notable interest are the wide main street, the picturesque 17th-century yarn market, the 15th-century church and the medieval castle on top of the hill. It is often open to the public in the summer, please check opening times. A short walk to Grabbist Hall offers delightful views of the surrounding area.

Like host like guest.

Wishing Well Tea Rooms

The Cliffs, Cheddar
Telephone: (01934) 742142

After a visit to the spectacular Cheddar Gorge enjoy simple but appetizing fare at this family-run tea room. Service is attentive and the atmosphere friendly – but in the the high season it does get very busy!
What to see:
Cheddar is famed for its gorge, caves and of course, cheeses. The area is magnificent but is best visited out of high season. As well as the caves do not omit to explore the upper gorge, often neglected by visitors to the area. There are good nature trails around Cheddar. It is fascinating to ponder how many other caves may exist, as yet, undiscovered.

Where love is, faith is.

THE TEA:
Delicious home-baked goodies like Dunster tutti frutti, Somerset cider cake and Bramley apple cake are always available, as are various set teas. Price: from £2.25.

OPEN:
Daily 10.00am to 6.00pm. Closed weekdays November to Christmas and all of January to March.

GETTING THERE:
Dunster is on the A396 and A39 roads. Nearest motorway M5. Street parking.

THE TEA:
Plain, cream or fruit teas are served together with home-made cakes, shortbread and biscuits and a fresh brew of tea. Price: set tea from £3.

OPEN:
April to mid-October: daily 10.00am to 6.00pm. Closed weekdays mid-October to March, and all of December and January.

GETTING THERE:
Cheddar is on the A371. Nearest motorway M5. Parking in the village.

THE TEA:

What was once the decorating workshop has become the place for a tea break. The menu is modest but satisfying, soups, freshly made sandwiches together with warmed scones and slices of cake will jump-start the taste buds. Price: from £2.50.

OPEN:

The museum is open most of the year, the tearoom during the season, Monday to Saturday 10.00am to 4.00pm. Some Sundays. Please check as the times are subject to change.

GETTING THERE:

Longton is on the A50 Stoke-On-Trent road. Nearest motorway M6. Parking.

Moderation in all things.

THE TEA:

Forget that calories exist, and linger over home-made lemon meringue pie, or warm date and walnut sponge topped with dollops of cream, plus a variety of other favourite cakes and tarts. Good choices of tea. Price: cream tea from £3.

OPEN:

Four days a week-Tuesday, Wednesday, Friday and Saturday from 10.00am to 5.00pm. All year round.

GETTING THERE:

Leek is on the A53 A523 roads. Nearest motorway M6. Parking in the town.

Gladstone Pottery Museum

Longton
Telephone: (01782) 319232

This museum has been created in a preserved 19th-century pottery with cobbled yard and four enormous bottle shaped kilns. Craftsmen and women use Victorian equipment to demonstrate the traditional skills of the Staffordshire potters. Displays and exhibits tell the story of the people who once worked here.

What to see:

Alton Towers is nearby, and also such other great houses and gardens as Drayton Manor Park, Haddon Hall, Sudbury, Shugborough and Tutbury Castle. For anyone interested in our mining past a visit to Chatterley Whitfield museum is a fascinating experience.

Greystones

Stockwell Street, Leek
Telephone: (01538) 398522

Inside, an old stone-flagged floor leads to a charming parlour with beams, panelling, stained glass windows and a fire whispering in the grate when it's chilly. Greystones wraps homely hospitality around you like a favourite blanket. The sort of place to which you will want to potter back.

What to see:

Spend some time wandering around this interesting little town, it has many galleries antique and mill shops to poke about in. North west of Leek there are country roads to explore where you will encounter few other travellers. Head for the Cheshire border and the summit of The Old Man of Mow for outstanding views across the county.

A penny for your thoughts.

Marsh Farm Tea Rooms

Uttoxeter Road, Abbots Bromley
Telephone: (01283) 840323

A working farm provides an unusual setting for afternoon tea. The tea room is attractive and cosy, the welcome friendly and everything is home-made. It is sometimes advisable to book.
What to see:
Abbots Bromley is a charming village of old black and white houses, a church and an old butter cross. It is renowned for an ancient custom – the Horn Dance, performed annually in September. The dancers' costumes and horns are stored in the church where they may be viewed at various times.

THE TEA:
The menu offers freshly made sandwiches and salads, cakes and tarts made with free range eggs and delicious scones with jam and cream. There is a small choice of teas. Price: from £3.

OPEN:
Saturday, Sunday and Bank Holidays, April to October from 3.00 to 6.00pm. Closed October to Easter.

GETTING THERE:
Abbots Bromley is on the B5014 and B5234 roads. Nearest motorways M6 and M42. Own car park.

He that love the tree, loves the branch.

Passiflora

Stafford Street, Brewood
Telephone: (01902) 851557

You never know what you might find browsing at this tranquil spot: it could be anything from a an art deco teapot to an old perfume bottle. Afterwards, you don't have to endure the palava of finding something wholesome on a plate, just walk on through to the conservatory complete with wicker chairs and potted palms. The garden is tremendously agreeable on a warm summer's day
What to see:
The village once had a thriving market promoted by the local bishop: note the cluster of streets and houses round the church and market place. The Shropshire Union Canal skirts the village and close by are Boscobel House and Chillington Hall, please check for opening times.

Never refuse a good offer.

THE TEA:
The menu is short and to the point: spicy toasted teacakes, slices of yummy pies and cake flirtations such as banana and apricot. It goes without saying that the place has a sizeable selection of teas. Price: from £3.50.

OPEN:
Monday to Saturday, 9.30am to 5.00pm Early closing Wednesday at 1.00pm. Open Sunday, 2-5.00pm in summer only.

GETTING THERE:
Brewood is west of Cannock on the A5. Nearest motorways M6 M54. Parking in the village.

THE TEA:

The pastries are tempting and the scones, often straight from the oven, come with lashings of cream, and good choices of tea. Price: from £3. 'Families welcome, children and grannies adored' is the fitting motto!

OPEN:

Monday to Saturday from 10.00am to 5.00pm. Closed Sunday and Bank Holidays.

GETTING THERE:

Stafford is on the A34 road. Nearest motorway M6. Parking in the town.

---<o>---

He that has time has life.

---<o>---

THE TEA:

The real feather in Teazzells cap is its food. Sample good home cooking and baking with firm favourites and local specialities , like the Eccleshall biscuit, on the menu. It has quite a good line up of teas. Price: from £3.

OPEN:

Monday to Sunday from 9.30am to 5.00pm. All year round.

GETTING THERE:

Eccleshall is on the A519 and A5013 roads. Nearest motorway M6. Parking in the town.

Soup Kitchen

Church Lane, Stafford
Telephone: (01785) 54775

The star of Stafford without a shadow of a doubt is the Soup Kitchen, a 16th-century building with a warren of cosy corners inside. On dark, rainswept afternoons, or any other for that matter, there is no better way to spend a happy hour than to be seated here, taking tea, with someone you'd like to kiss.

What to see:

The church of Saint Mary's has a great octagonal tower, not often seen in England, a 13th-century interior and a bust of Izzak Walton, who was christened here. Even the industrial parts of the county are of interest because much of it has been conserved and is, surprisingly, picturesque.

---<o>---

Teazzells Tea Rooms

High Street, Eccleshall
Telephone: (01785) 851918

This is a jolly place, morning or afternoon for a drink, a light snack or enjoying the 'happy hour' – that is, 4.00pm. The building is a 19th-century warren with any number of rooms, one of which is a gallery. Local artists display their paintings and there are crafts and gifts to thumb through.

What to see:

The medieval bishops built one of the most perfect 13th-century churches in the county and merits a visit. The castle is privately owned, but opens on occasions. The High Street is lined with 18th- and 19th-century shops and houses. Within driving distance are Haddon Hall, Shugborough and Tutbury Castle.

---<o>---

A full cup must be carried steadily.

---<o>---

Old Post Office Tea Room

Alstonefield, nr. Ashbourne
Telephone: (01335) 310201

Just off the A515, the traveller may chance upon a charming 17th-century house which, to his/her delight, will turn out to be a tea room. The Old Post Office is a very homely place, known for its collection of odd cups and saucers and is a favourite with local people and tourists alike.

What to see:

On the borders of Derbyshire and Staffordshire the surrounding countryside is not only beautiful but varied and well worth exploring. Ashbourne lies near the Matlocks, a group of towns and villages in the Derwent valley. Matlock Bath (once a spa) is both picturesque and interesting.

THE TEA:
There are always choices on the tea menu, which features home-made scones, biscuits, tarts, cakes and crumbles. The preserves and jam are very popular and can be bought to take home. There is a selection of teas. Price: from £3.

OPEN:
Thursday to Tuesday 10.30am to 5.00pm mid March to November. Closed Wednesday. Summer months, open daily.

GETTING THERE:
Alstonefield is north of Ashbourne on the A515. Nearest motorways M1 and M6. Parking in the village.

A pennyweight of love is worth a pound of law.

Whitmore Gallery Tea Room

Keele Lane, Whitmore
Telephone: (01782) 680879

Originally built as a 17th-century coaching inn on the busy Liverpool to Birmingham run, this delightful old house is now run as a friendly informal gallery and tea room. There's a lovely assortment of contemporary paintings and pottery and a good selection of knitwear, all for sale.

What to see:

The church in Whitmore is one of only several half-timbered churches in the county and has an unusual wooden bell turret dating from 1632. Newcastle-under-Lyme has a good museum and art gallery in Brampton Park where ancient charters, dating from the 13th century, are on display.

Travel makes a wise man better.

THE TEA:
For tea there are freshly made sandwiches, and some splendid home-baking to enjoy, with goodies like scones, oatcakes, crumpets and chocolate and lemon cakes served with a choice of tea blends. Price: from £2.50.

OPEN:
Monday to Sunday 10.00am to 6.00pm. Closed Christmas and New Year.

GETTING THERE:
Whitmore is south-west of Newcastle-under-Lyme on the A53. Nearest motorway M6. Street parking and town car park.

THE TEA:

The chocolate ganache and the hot lemon Madeira cake are definitely worth making a detour for! Set teas are also served including afternoon tea at around £4.00, offered with a fine selection of teas.

OPEN:

Monday to Saturday 9.30am to about 6.00pm. Sunday: 10.00am to 5.00pm.

GETTING THERE:

Bury St Edmunds is situated on the main A45. Parking is limited, and controlled, in the busy town centre.

The sun has stood still but time never did.

THE TEA:

No hard decisions to make here. Relax and partake of some little cakes, cream teas and various light snacks served with a choice of teas. Price: cream teas from £2.50.

OPEN:

Daily from 10.00am to 5.30pm during the summer months. Same times in winter, but please check.

GETTING THERE:

Long Melford is on the A134. Own car park and plentiful parking in the main street.

Bailey's Restaurant and Tea Room

5 Whiting Street, Bury St Edmunds
Telephone: (01284) 706198

This small, intimate restaurant and tea room is to be found in one of Bury's quaint, narrow streets close to the town centre. Simple cane chairs and plain china make for an easy-going charm. You will receive friendly service from the smiling staff, and altogether it is an enjoyable experience!

What to see:

Bury St Edmunds is a thriving cathedral town with much of historic interest. It is essentially Georgian, but Moyse's Hall, now an excellent museum, dates from the 12th century and the abbey ruins from the 13th century. It is best to discover Bury on foot.

Carousel

White Hart Antique Centre, Long Melford
Telephone: (01787) 311511

Hands up those of you who enjoy nothing better than scouring antique shops? If you have been searching for odd sized baking tins, antique linens and old furniture, you need look no more. You'll find them all at the White Hart Antique Centre. When you're ready to take a breather, you can have a bite to eat in the tiny tea room.

What to see:

With its large green and parish church, Long Melford has the atmosphere of a village rather than a town. Worth a visit are the 15th century Holy Trinity church and Long Melford Hall visited by Queen Elizabeth I in 1578. Not forgetting the innumerable curio shops and antique centres.

That's my good that does me good.

Curtis's

High Street, Southwold
Telephone: (01502) 724077

In this pleasant tea shop, overlooking the High Street at the front, and a small courtyard garden at the back, a relaxed and friendly atmosphere prevails. The tea is good and the staff are very helpful.

What to see:
Southwold is part of Suffolk's heritage coast, now carefully preserved as an area of outstanding beauty. It stretches from Lowestoft in the north of the county to the Victorian resort of Felixstowe in the south. The sea constantly erodes the coast, and this can be seen most graphically at Dunwich where the medieval port has been lost to the tides. Southwold has a fine 15th-century church and a charming local museum.

THE TEA:
Teatime brings home-made cakes and sponges as well as set cream teas, served with well made pots of tea – Earl Grey or Darjeeling are the choices. Price: from £2.60.

OPEN:
Monday to Saturday 3.00 to 5.00pm. Closed Sunday.

GETTING THERE:
Southwold is on the A1095 off the A12. Street parking in the town.

At a round table, there's no dispute of place.

The Granary

Snape Maltings, Snape
Telephone: (01728) 688 303

Beside the River Alde, Snape Maltings is a unique collection of Victorian industrial buildings, originally used to malt barley. The centre includes unusual shops, galleries and the tea room known as The Granary.

What to see:
Snape Maltings is the home of the world famous Aldeburgh Festival started by the English composer Benjamin Britten in 1948 and held each year in June. As well as the June Festival the concert hall is used for many performances throughout the year. There are river trips on the Alde during the summer, and close by is the attractive seaside town of Aldeburgh.

THE TEA:
Cakes, pastries and home-made scones are available from the self service counter, as are pots of Darjeeling, Earl Grey or camomile tea. On sunny days tea can be enjoyed on a grassy area outside. Price: from £2.

OPEN:
Daily 10.00am to 5.00pm.

GETTING THERE:
Snape is on the B1094 off the A12. The site has a large car park.

Appetite comes with eating.
F Rabelais

Dear Ms Cress

Thank you very much for your letter about tea. I am
certainly a tea drinker. I take it in the morning
with my breakfast and again in the afternoon, either
at 4.00.pm. or 5.00.pm. I never drink Indian tea and
it would horrify me to drink Darjeeling. The only tea
I ever choose is Earl Grey, although I am prepared to
put up with Lapsang Soochong if Earl Grey is not
available.

Yours sincerely

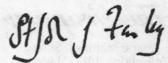

Mill Hotel

Walnut Tree Lane, Sudbury
Telephone: (01787) 375544

Full square on Walnut Tree Lane it stands: a handsome, white, solid building. The rooms inside are of a piece, with low ceilings, stone floors and an air of Suffolk gentility and commitment to serious respectability. That is not to say that the Mill is stuffy! Plenty of space, easy going service good homely food: result, contentment all round.
What to see:
Gainsborough was born in the town, and his house is open to the public. There are a number of Georgian and older buildings. The weaving tradition continues (Princess Di's silk wedding dress was woven here); and some medieval weavers cottages still exist. It is a lively town, which hosts many varied events throughout the year. Within easy reach are Bury St Edmunds, Colchester and Ipswich.

THE TEA:
Take tea in the comfortable bar-lounge, note the old millwheel; or in the garden that leads down to the banks of the River Stour. There are always freshly made sandwiches, scones and cakes on the menu to accompany a good choice of teas. Price: from £4.

OPEN:
Daily from 3-5.00pm for tea.

GETTING THERE:
Sudbury is on the A131 and A134 roads. Own car park.

Great hopes make great men.

Mary's

Walberswick
Telephone: (01502) 723243

Inside Mary's are reminders of how close Walberswick is to the sea; fishing nets are draped over walls and ceilings, sea shells line the window sills and pictures of boats adorn the walls. In good weather the garden provides a pleasant setting for tea.
What to see:
Although once a prosperous Suffolk town, Walberswick is now a small resort, with good sailing facilities and bracing walks to take along the coast and across the heaths. There is a Heritage Coast Visitor Centre on the Green, with detailed information about Suffolk's coast.

THE TEA:
There's always a varied selection of home-made cakes, as well as cream and high teas accompanied by Assam, Earl Grey or Darjeeling tea. Price: from £3.25.

OPEN:
Easter to October: Tuesday to Sunday 10.00am to 6.00pm. Closed Monday except Bank Holidays. November to Easter: open Friday and weekends only.

GETTING THERE:
Walberswick is on the B1387 off the A12. Own car park.

Cooks are not to be taught in their own kitchen.

THE TEA:
Feast on soups, light snacks and savouries such as: Welsh rarebit or potted shrimps. Cream teas and home-made cakes are popular in the afternoons. Sunday promises a roast. Price: from £3.50 for tea.

OPEN:
Daily from 10.00am to 6.00pm March to October. In winter, weekends only, 10.00am to 5.00pm.

GETTING THERE:
Orford is signposted off the A12 on the B1084 or B1078. Parking in the village.

No, thank you has lost many a good butter cake. Proverb.

THE TEA:
Weave your way through some very appealing cakes and slices, or slice into a 'tickled pink' cream tea. Tea initiatives comprise Earl Grey, Darjeeling, and common or garden. Price: from £4.

OPEN:
Monday to Saturday from 10.00am to 5.00pm. Sunday to 5.30pm.

GETTING THERE:
Lavenham is on the A1141. Nearest motorway M11. Parking in the village.

Quietness is a great treasure.

The Old Warehouse

The Quay, Orford
Telephone: (01394) 450210

Sail boats and fishing boats bob up and down on the water at Orford and sea gulls wheel in the breezy blue and white sky. The salty, fresh air inevitably leaves visitors feeling ravenous and close to the quay stands a fine old warehouse, with tea rooms on the ground floor. The atmosphere is informal and the staff are easy-going.

What to see:
The fine keep is all that remains of Orford castle commissioned by Henry II. There are splendid views from the top. Inland lies another magnificent castle at Framlingham. Southwold and Aldeburgh are two more relatively unspoilt seaside towns. Though in summer, music lovers are drawn to the annual festival at Aldeburgh.

Tickle Manor Tea Rooms

High Street, Lavenham
Telephone: (01787) 248438

Cameras and camcorders are everywhere in the lovely village of Lavenham, setting for many a half-timbered TV drama and romance for that matter. Pick your starting point and, once there, you can meander far and wide-confidently recording. Later you can drop in on Tickle Manor for the backbone of any afternoon – a rippling tea.

What to see:
It's hard to imagine that anyone who has made the journey to Lavenham has gone away disappointed, in fact were it not for the traffic, the visitor could well imagine that he or she had been transported back to the Middle Ages. Visit the Guildhall and the splendid church. Other classic villages to visit are Clare and Cavendish.

Aster's Tea Shop

Middle Street, Shere
Telephone: (01483) 202445

Amidst the gentle folds of Surrey's Downs a number of picturesque villages lie hidden, nestling amongst them is Shere. In the centre of the village stands the tea shop. One steps into a comfortable Victorian style tea room with cream walls and mellow pine furniture.

What to see:
This beautiful old village has one of Surrey's most interesting Norman churches, half-timbered houses, stone cottages, a stream and an old cornmill. It is best visited in the Spring or early Autumn. Visit the Silent Pool, one mile to the west.

THE TEA:
Aster's has a simple menu with choices of various set teas, as well as sandwiches, cakes and pastries served with Earl Grey, Darjeeling, Ceylon and Lapsang Souchong blends. Price: from £3.50.

OPEN:
Tuesday to Friday 10.00am to 5.30pm. Weekends 10.00am to 6.00pm. Weekends and Bank Holidays set teas only.

GETTING THERE:
Shere is signposted off the A25, A248 Guildford to Dorking road. Parking is permitted in the village.

Every one to his taste.

Gomshall Mill

Gomshall
Telephone: (01483) 202433

The white, weatherboarded watermill stretches across the trout-filled waters of the Tillingbourne, an ancient building on a site where a mill already existed at the time of the Domesday Book. One part of it is shops, and there is an especially distinctive tea room. Tea is served in the granary and it is all you might expect: flagged floors and ceilings and walls of brick and wood. The old, wooden settles and tables really add to the charm.

What to see:
The village is pleasant to explore on foot, and whether you walk or drive, the surrounding countryside is very attractive.

THE TEA:
The choices of tea may include brown bread and butter or a slice of fruit loaf; scones with butter and a home-made cake or two, served with Indian or China tea. Price: £3.50.

OPEN:
Monday to Sunday 10.00am to 5.30pm. After 3.00pm Saturday, Sunday and Bank Holidays set teas only are served.

GETTING THERE:
Gomshall is situated on the A25 between Guildford and Dorking. Car park at the Mill.

Kindness comes of will.

135

Joyce's-on-the-Chart

Limpsfield Chart
Telephone: (01883) 722195

The appeal of Joyce's-on-the-Chart is immediate. One steps into what was the old village bakehouse, complete with faggot oven, all now charmingly restored. On fine days guests take tea in the pretty cottage garden and often don't want to leave!

What to see:
Don't confuse Limpsfield and Limpsfield Chart. Limpsfield is a charming village with many old buildings. Limpsfield Chart lies in a scenic area of woodland known as the High Chart – superb walking and driving country, at its best in May and October.

He who is contented enjoys.

Manor Farm Craft Centre

Seale, Farnham
Telephone: (01252) 783333

Though hardly off the beaten track – it stands on the A31 – Manor Farm could easily be missed as one sped by, on the way to or from Guildford. It is a good place to break a journey, have a look around and enjoy a cup of tea in what was the old milking dairy.

What to see:
The Castle, formerly the seat of the bishops of Winchester, dominates the town and the keep is open to the public. The Wilmer House museum is devoted to local history and William Cobbett relics – he was born in Farnham in 1763, and buried in the local church .

An Englishman's home is his castle.

THE TEA:
The home-baking selection is very impressive, ranging from shortbread to irresistible wedges of cake, to super scones with real jam. A choice of teas includes Indian, China, fruit and herbal. Price: set tea from £3.

OPEN:
Monday, Tuesday, Wednesday and Friday, Winter: 2.00 to 4.00pm. Summer: 3.00 to 6.00pm. Weekends and Bank Holidays 3.00 to 6.00pm all year round, set teas only. Closed Thursday.

GETTING THERE:
Limpsfield Chart is off the B269. Nearest motorway M25. Car parking in the village.

THE TEA:
Cheery, informal service and a selection of home-baked produce including scones, slices, chocolate and walnut cakes are all on the menu. Indian, Earl Grey, fruit and camomile are the tea choices. Price: a cream tea from £$2.75.

OPEN:
Tuesday to Saturday 10.00am to 5.00pm, from 2.30pm for tea, Sunday and Bank Holidays 2.00 to 5.00pm. Closed Monday.

GETTING THERE:
Seale is signposted off the A31. Nearest motorways M3 and M25. Ample car parking.

Original Maids of Honour Tearooms

Kew Road, Kew
Telephone: (0181) 940 2752

A cosy, crowded, traditional tea room, which when sighted through the window seems to be wrapped in a soft pink haze! The speciality is a pastry called 'Maid of Honour'. The story goes that a cook created the pastry especially for King Henry VIII and the recipe, which is a well-guarded secret, has been passed down through the centuries to the Newens family.

What to see:
Kew is renowned the world over for its botanical gardens. Visitors can spend a day exploring over three hundred acres of woodland, lakes and flower plantations. There is a Pagoda erected in 1761, and Kew Palace has relics of George III.

THE TEA:
A set tea of wonderfully light scones, with the usual accompaniments, and a serving of home-made cakes for you to decide upon. A small array of teas completes the setting. Price: set tea £4.20.

OPEN:
Daily 9.00am to 5.00pm. Closed Monday afternoon and Sunday.

GETTING THERE:
Nearest tube Kew Gardens. There's parking for cars.

First try and then trust.

Watts Gallery Tea Room

Compton, near Guildford.
Telephone: (01483) 811030 (not mealtimes)

A couple of minutes walk away from the beautiful unusual Watts Gallery is this very friendly tea room. In good weather tables are moved out into the garden, while inside tea drinkers sit at comfortable tables beneath the old rafters.

What to see:
The gallery is devoted to the works of the Victorian painter George Frederick Watts. On exhibit here are about 200 of his works. His wife, the painter Mary Fraser-Tytler, designed the nearby Watts mortuary chapel. Altogether a charming and most interesting place to visit. Do check the gallery opening times.

He who travels far knows much.

THE TEA:
All the cakes, scones, savouries and preserves are home-cooked using traditional ingredients, methods and free range eggs. A lively selection of teas includes Indian, Ceylon, China and herbal, the menu always features a tea-of-the-month. Price: a Compton tea from £3.

OPEN:
Monday to Sunday 10.30am to 5.30pm. Closed Christmas week and New Year.

GETTING THERE:
Compton is on the B3000 just off the A3. Nearest motorway M25. Ample car parking.

April Cottage Tea Room

Mayfield
Telephone: (01435) 872160

East Sussex has its share of traditional tea rooms, but few are as old as April Cottage, an intimate Tudor cottage tucked away on a side turning in the village of Mayfield. Inside, the tea room is cool and rustic, with white-washed walls, beams, a fireplace that stretches the width of the room and classic dark wood tables and chairs. At teatime, the freshly prepared set teas are all delicious.

What to see:
A walk around the village is most worthwhile. There are views of the Weald and South Downs, the Church dates from the early 17th century, and the Archbishops of Canterbury once had a palace here.

THE TEA:
A choice of set teas including a full afternoon tea of bread and butter, cakes, scones, jam and cream with a pot of tea is priced at £2.75.

OPEN:
Daily 3.00 to 5.30pm. Closed Christmas and New Year.

GETTING THERE:
Mayfield is eight miles south of Tunbridge Wells on the A267. Car parking in the village.

A little house well filled.

Exceat Farmhouse

Exceat, 7 Sisters Country Park, Seaford
Telephone: (01323) 870218

This 17th-century farmhouse nestles in the heart of the sheltered Cuckmere Valley. Everything on offer at this tremendously agreeable tea house, with its own garden courtyard, is made on the premises. The atmosphere is peaceful and the service friendly.

What to see:
The country park runs down to the sea by the River Cuckmere, protected meadow, saltings, shingle and chalk headlands are the features. Popular sights in the county of East Sussex include Michelham Priory, Battle Abbey, Pevensey Castle and the picturesque village of Alfriston. Inland, a major attraction is the Ashdown Forest, part forest and part heathland.

THE TEA:
The menu includes scones with clotted cream, muffins, crumpets and a rich variety of cakes and biscuits. For those without a sweet tooth savoury snacks and sandwiches are also available. Price: from £3.50.

OPEN:
Daily opening from 10.00am to 6.00pm. Winter earlier closing at 4.30pm. Also open some Friday and Saturday evenings. Please check.

GETTING THERE:
The farmhouse and park are signposted off the A259, Seaford-Eastbourne road. Nearest motorway M23. Car park.

Provision in season makes a rich house.

Beam Ends

Hedgers Hill, Walberton
Telephone: (01243) 551254

Comfort, quiet, discretion and seductive grub are the timeless ingredients for this classic English cottage. The pleasure of finding a place like Beam Ends, is that it offers a welcoming solace from the often cruel world outside. On fine days the garden is the place to escape to.

What to see:

Arundel Castle, with its Norman gates, barbican and keep, is the greatest of Sussex castles. Viewed from across the River Arun it still presents a fairytale vision of an authentic medieval stronghold. As in many other respects, Sussex is rich in the variety and beauty of its houses, ranging from small medieval manor houses to fine Georgian houses to magical castles.

THE TEA:
The menu chimes perfectly with the place itself. There are daily hot specials and light lunches. Sandwiches are freshly made and scones, pies and cakes are all handled with great care.
Price from £3.50.

OPEN:
Tuesday to Sunday from 11.00am to 5.30pm summer opening. In winter open some weekends but closed all of January. Please check.

GETTING THERE:
Walberton is signposted off the B2132. Car parking is possible.

A little with quiet is the only diet.

Sussex (East)

The Tudor House

High Street, Alfriston
Telephone: (01323) 870891

A mellowed 14th century building with many original features, The Tudor House stands in the main street of this picturesque village. The two rooms, for taking tea, are peaceful and traditional in character whilst, in the summer, the pleasant garden with views over the Downs is an inviting setting in which to enjoy some refreshment.

What to see:

Alfriston is an extremely interesting village, with timbered houses and winding streets, and there are endless things to do and see, the Sussex Downs, the village green, the 14th-century church, and much more besides.

A friend is never known till needed.

THE TEA:
You can sample either a Sussex cream tea or items from an a la carte selection of savouries, sandwiches, scones and a range of cakes from shortbread to gateaux. There is a choice of tea blends.
Price: from £3.

OPEN:
Monday to Sunday from 10.00am to 5.30pm. Closed over the Christmas holiday.

GETTING THERE:
Alfriston is well signposted off the A27. There is a car park in the village.

Chaunt House Tea Rooms

High Street, Burwash
Telephone: (01435) 882221

The picture-postcard village of Burwash is instantly captivating, and positively invites a meander through its gentle old streets; Chaunt House sits comfortably in the middle. It's the kind of place that makes you feel instantly at home. The sedate ticking and chiming of the various period clocks is certain to have you pouring tea with a smile!

What to see:
Burwash is an attractive tile-hung village, with a church dating from the 12th century. Outside the village is Bateman's, Rudyard Kipling's home for more than thirty years. Please check opening times.

THE TEA:

Delicious multi-layered cakes, scones and gateaux, all baked by owner Milly, are certain to ensure sweet dreams and fond memories. Teas served include Darjeeling and Earl Grey. Price: £2.50.

OPEN:

Tuesday to Saturday 10.00am to 5.30pm, Sunday 2.30 to 5.30pm. Closed Monday and for one month from Christmas Eve to the end of January.

GETTING THERE:

Burwash is situated on the A265. Parking is permitted in the village.

A good wife and health is a man's best wealth.

Knollys

Bodiam
Telephone: (01580) 830323

After looking around the castle and gardens, a visit to the tea room is a must – particularly if you hanker after a slice of home-made chocolate cake! Next door is an attractive craft and gift shop. Service is friendly and cheerful.

What to see:
Bodiam is a small village with a great 14th-century castle standing in a lily-filled moat. It was built to withstand French invasions and the outer walls of this magnificent castle are almost intact. Floors have been replaced in two towers and it is possible to climb the circular stairs and enjoy views of the surrounding countryside.

THE TEA:

Fresh cream cakes, chocolate cake, and Victoria sponges are all freshly baked for teatime. There are also cream and high teas. Prices from £4. Teas served include China, Early Grey, Assam and Darjeeling.

OPEN:

Easter until mid October daily 10.30am to 5.00pm.

GETTING THERE:

Bodiam is on the A229. Limited parking in the village. Car park in the castle grounds.

Be just before you are generous.

The Mock Turtle

4 Pool Valley, Brighton
Telephone: (01273) 327380

After touring the 'Lanes', wander down the narrow streets to find The Mock Turtle. The atmosphere is most convivial and there are so many varieties of cakes and breads that you'll lose count. It's deservedly popular with regulars and visitors alike!

What to see:
Brighton came to prominence in the 18th century when a Dr Russell proclaimed the medicinal value of sea bathing. In 1783 the Prince of Wales, later George VI, paid one of many visits, and the town was set to become fashionable. Today it is the largest resort in the South East and offers something for everyone.

THE TEA:
The display features wonderful cakes, flapjacks, teabreads and light fluffy scones with home-made preserve. There is a range of good teas. Price: from £3.

OPEN:
Tuesday to Saturday 10 00am to 6.00pm. Closed Sunday, Monday, Christmas and two weeks in the autumn.

GETTING THERE:
Brighton is on the A23 and A237 roads. Nearest motorway M23 Meter parking and public car parks.

A small gift is better than a great promise.

The Old Post House

Offham, near Lewes
Telephone: (01273) 477358

The Old Post House – originally part of the Shiffner estate, was the village shop for over a hundred years, and is a Grade II listed building. It is now a comfortable family run tea room in a romantic setting – the garden overlooks two churches, Offham Church built in 1860 and the Norman Hamsey Church dating from the 12th century.

What to see:
The village churches. Also Glyndebourne, established in 1934 as a summer festival of music, the opera season is now internationally renowned. Lewes is a pleasant, unrushed country town.

THE TEA:
One could have tea here three or four times a week – it has been known – and still leave wanting more! All the baking is memorable for its imagination and flavour Price: from £2.

OPEN:
Saturday and Sunday from 2 00 to 6.00pm throughout the year

GETTING THERE:
Offham is just north of Lewes on the A275. There is a car park in the lane by the church.

Old friends and old wine are best.

Patricia,

I hope that I have a minimum of major vices : I don't drink or smoke or infringe on the severer commandments. However I have to confess to a major indulgence : tea. I am positively obsessed with it. The mere thought, let alone taste, of a steaming cup of tea will send the pulse racing faster than any gymnastics could induce. It stimulates the start of the day and effectuates that moment of calm equipoise between the working and the relaxing day — that endearing ritual called tea-time. (The more snobbish and exact French have even pin-pointed its precise timing — "le fif o'clock"!)

With all best wishes,

yours ev,

Shepherd's Tea Rooms

35 Little London, Chichester
Telephone: (01243) 774761

A relaxed and friendly atmosphere prevails at this pleasant, well run tea shop, in the heart of Chichester. Using only the best ingredients, cakes and tea are served from pretty china, on tables covered with lace cloths.

What to see:
An ancient city, Chichester has a beautiful Norman Cathedral, a market cross, old Assembly Rooms and the modern Festival theatre. The harbour is renowned as a boating centre and water tours are available. Two miles west at Fishbourne is the Roman Palace, Britain's largest Roman building.

THE TEA:
The lightest of scones come with fruit loaves and a mouth watering selection of cakes, from chocolate eclairs to crisp meringues. A good choice of teas is available. Price from £2.95.

OPEN:
Monday to Saturday 9.00am to 5.00pm. Closed Sunday.

GETTING THERE:
Chichester is on the A27, A286, A259 and A285 roads. Nearest motorway M27 Public and pay and display car parks.

*When I makes tea,
I makes tea
As old Mother Grogan
said.. – James Joyce*

St Martin's Tea Rooms

St Martin's Street, Chichester
Telephone: (01243) 786715

This is a charming tea room close to the city centre. The building is medieval in origin but with an 18th-century facade typical of many of the city's historic, terraced houses. It also has a small, pretty brick-paved garden for summer teas.

What to see:
The county town of West Sussex, Chichester is also a cathedral town. The city's history dates back to Roman times, but it is renowned for its Georgian buildings particularly in a street called Little London. The cathedral is mainly Norman, and the Lady Chapel contains some of the oldest work.

THE TEA:
The aim of the tea room is to provide healthy foods, using organic, natural, unrefined wholefoods wherever possible. The tea menu is simple offering scones, shortbread and honey and fruit cakes. Herbal, fruit and caffeine free teas are available. Price: from £3.

OPEN:
Tuesday to Saturday 10.00am to 6.00pm Closed Sunday and Monday, Christmas and New Year.

GETTING THERE:
Chichester is on the main A27 and A286 roads. Car parking restricted to the town's car parks.

*'Take some more tea' the March Hare said to Alice earnestly..
Lewis Carroll*

143

Swan Cottage Tea Rooms

41 The Mint, Rye
Telephone: (0797) 222423

The black and white, half-timbered Swan Cottage, which dates back to 1420, stands on the main street of Rye amidst ancient inns, potteries and antique shops. Inside there are two rooms for tea, the favourite, at the back, is white-walled and beamed with a large brick fireplace.

What to see:

Rye is worth a lingering visit to explore its cobbled lanes, antique shops and historic fortifications, for there are few towns where a medieval town plan and original houses have survived so little altered. Rye was the setting for E F Benson's Mapp and Lucia stories.

THE TEA:

As well as the pastries and cakes you will be offered a choice of set teas – one of which is the special Swan Cottage afternoon tea with a pot of Darjeeling, Earl Grey or Lapsang Souchong. Price: £4.50.

OPEN:

Wednesday to Monday 10.30am to 5.00pm. Closed Tuesday.

GETTING THERE:

Rye is situated on the A259, east of Hastings. Pay and display parking on the outskirts of the town.

In doing we learn.

The Willow Tea Room

84 All Saint's Street, Old Town, Hastings
Telephone: (01424) 430656

On one of those cold, grey seaside days – of which Hastings has its fair share – nothing lifts the spirits and warms the cockles of the heart like a generous serving of afternoon tea. The Willow Tea Room with its cheerful ambience is a favourite spot, minutes from the sea front in the Old Town.

What to see:

A traditional, family, seaside resort catering for all tastes. There is a museum of local history and the unique Shipwreck Heritage Centre, as well as Britain's first Norman Castle.

THE TEA:

A good choice is the Willow set tea of assorted sandwiches, scones, jam, cream and a slice of cake with a pot of tea. The tea list includes Indian, Ceylon, China and fruit. Price: £4.50.

OPEN:

Easter to September: Tuesday to Sunday 3.00 to 5.00pm. Closed Monday. October to Easter: Saturday and Sunday 3.00 to 6.00pm. Closed Monday to Friday.

GETTING THERE:

Hastings is reached on the A21. Parking is permitted along the sea front.

Take time when time comes.

Brethren's Kitchen

Lord Leycester Hospital, Warwick
Telephone: (01926) 491580

Part of the medieval Lord Leycester Hospital, founded by the Earl in 1571, the tea room has exposed beams and stone floors. It's easy to imagine monks dispensing hospitality to passing guests in this charming atmosphere.

What to see:
An ancient county town Warwick is renowned for its magnificent medieval castle. A fire in 1694 destroyed much of medieval Warwick but some buildings still remain. The church of St Mary dates from the 14th century and in the Beauchamp Chapel is the tomb of Richard, Earl of Warwick – prominent in the story of Joan of Arc.

THE TEA:
Scones with fresh cream, biscuits, sponge cakes, assorted slices and fruit cake are always available. A choice of tea blends include Indian, China and herbal. Price: from £2.20.

OPEN:
Tuesday to Sunday 10.00am to 5.00pm. Closed Monday and November to Easter.

GETTING THERE:
Warwick is on the A46 and A445 roads Nearest motorway M40. Own car park.

Make much of what you have.

Kerry House Tea Rooms

3 Market Place, Shipston-on-Stour
Telephone: (01608) 661733

Comfort, cheerful service and good value are the hallmarks of this family run tea room in the centre of Shipston-on-Stour. The shop is old, 18th-century, and traditional and offers good home-baking.

What to see:
Shipston has a number of interesting 17th- and 18th-century buildings. It makes an excellent centre for exploring the northern Cotswolds. Edgehilll, a four mile long ridge rims an early Civil War battlefield at Radway, Charles I claimed victory. A young Captain Oliver Cromwell learnt several lessons here! Upper Brailes has lovely views, and Lower Brailes a 14th-century church.

THE TEA:
Quality home-made pastries, fruit pies, and cakes can be enjoyed throughout the afternoon, with a choice of Indian or China tea. Price from £2.50

OPEN:
Monday to Saturday 9.00am to 5.00pm. Closed Sunday.

GETTING THERE:
Shipston-on-Stour is on the A34 Nearest motorway M40 Street parking

A little kitchen makes a large house.

THE TEA:

Teatime treats include gateaux, pastries, teacakes and a very filling cream tea. There is a choice of tea blends. Price: from £3.50.

OPEN:

Monday to Sunday 9.30am until late, particularly in the summer months.

GETTING THERE:

Stratford-upon-Avon is on the A34, A422 and A439 roads. Nearest motorway M40. Street and car parking.

Do nothing but eat, and make good cheer and praise heaven for the merry year.
– William Shakespeare

THE TEA:

There will be cakes and pastries such as chocolate roulade, strawberry Pavlova, raspberry and almond slices and warmed scones. The tea list is excellent. Price: from £4.

OPEN:

Monday to Saturday 9.30am to 5.30pm, Sunday 10.30am to 5.30pm.

GETTING THERE:

Bradford-on-Avon is on the A363. Nearest motorway M4. Public car parks.

Mistress Quickly

Henley Street, Stratford-upon-Avon
Telephone: (01789) 295261

Across the street from the birthplace of Shakespeare, is this attractive and busy tea room. All the cakes and pastries are made on the premises and are served by willing staff.

What to see:

In Stratford, visitors usually begin by visiting Shakespeare's birthplace in Henley Street and his grave in Holy Trinity church. New Place is the house where he eventually settled and wrote 'The Tempest'. Hall's Croft was the home of his daughter and her husband. His wife's childhood home, Anne Hathaway's Cottage, is in nearby Shottery. Best visited in late Spring and early Autumn.

Wiltshire
Bridge Tea Rooms

24a Bridge Street, Bradford-on-Avon
Telephone: (0122586) 5537

The ambience at the Bridge Tea Rooms is one of subdued sophistication. The decor is Victorian – old photographs, antique furniture and working fireplaces, even the staff are authentically dressed! The food – elegant and flavoursome, nicely complements the above.

What to see:

Bradford-on-Avon is a most delightful stone-built hillside town. An old bridge crosses the river and in the centre is a tiny lock-up, originally a chapel. Also a small Saxon chapel was rediscovered in the 19th century, while close by is an old tithe barn, and much else besides. This is a place in which to linger.

I have been toiling and moiling for the prettiest piece of china, my dear.
– William Wycherley

Audrey's Tea Room

55 High Street, Corsham
Telephone: (01249) 714931

Here the traditional English tea room still exists, a delight for surprised visitors and a favourite venue for local residents throughout the year. If you are passing through Corsham you are recommended to stop and sample the homely hospitality that you will discover here.

What to see:
Corsham is a small, 18th-century town built handsomely of Bath stone. The church is of interest and close by is Corsham Court, a fine house built over the 16th–18th centuries. Please check opening times. The county of Wiltshire has many listed buildings, attractive villages and prehistoric sites.

That which is well done is twice done.

THE TEA:
A simple menu of scones and some uncomplicated, home-made cakes is supplemented by a range of sandwiches and light snacks. A choice of tea blends is offered. Price: from £3.

OPEN:
Monday to Saturday from 9.00am to 2.00pm and from 3.00 to 5.00pm. Throughout the year. Closed Sunday (except in Summer), Christmas and New Year holiday.

GETTING THERE:
Corsham is west of Chippenham on the A4. Nearest motorway M4. Parking in the town.

King John's Hunting Lodge

Lacock Village
Telephone: (01249) 730313

In the centre of this beautiful village, stands this centuries old stone cottage. You will find small, beamed rooms with polished tables and wooden chairs. The lodge is run with charm and civility.

What to see:
In Lacock's winding narrow streets are half timbered cottages, grey stone houses, the church of St Cyriac, a 14th-century medieval barn, and the abbey founded by Ela Countess of Salisbury, in 1229. After the dissolution, the abbey was converted into a mansion. In Victorian times Fox Talbot, the pioneer photographer, lived and worked here.

If with me you'll fondly stray over hills and far away. – John Gaye

THE TEA:
It offers a scone tea served with Jersey cream and preserve or local honey, as well as a good assortment of home-made cakes. All to be enjoyed with a choice of teas. Price: from £3.50.

OPEN:
April to November: Monday to Sunday 3.00 to around 6.00pm or later. Weekend throughout the year.

GETTING THERE:
Lacock is just off the A350 Melksham to Chippenham road. Nearest motorway M4. Village car park.

THE TEA:

Sample the special cream cakes, pastries and gateaux, all home-made, all mouth-watering. Look out for the good selection of teas. Price: cream tea from £3.00.

OPEN:

Monday to Saturday 9.00am to 5.30pm. Closed Sunday and Bank Holidays.

GETTING THERE:

Salisbury is on the A30, A36, and A338 roads Car park in town centre.

Hunger finds no fault with the cookery.

Michael Snell

8 St Thomas's Square, Salisbury
Telephone: (01722) 336037

Close to the centre of the city, this character tea room was once the old town miller's house to the front, and a former church school at the rear. You can sit either at the simple tables inside, or on warm days outside enjoying afternoon tea.

What to see:

Salisbury is a delightful city, buildings of all periods line the streets, medieval bridges span the river, and first sight of the cathedral is particularly impressive. Constable painted one of his famous pictures here. Samuel Pepys stayed a night, sleeping in a silken bed, and Nell Gwynne purchased scissors here. Perhaps the unhappiest visitor was the Duke of Buckingham – beheaded in 1485 by order of Richard III.

THE TEA:

There are good set afternoon teas, and sweet tooths can have a field day with a marvellous selection of cakes. There is a choice of teas. Price: from £4.

OPEN:

Monday to Friday 8.30am to 6.00pm, Saturday 8.00am to 7.00pm, Sunday 9.00am to 7.00pm Closed Christmas and New Year

GETTING THERE:

Marlborough is on the A4, street parking and car parks available.

The Polly Tea Rooms

High Street, Marlborough
Telephone: (01672) 512146

In Marlborough's charming high street is this traditional tea room. The bow windows, low beamed ceilings and pretty tableware create the right atmosphere for a delicious afternoon tea. It's extremely popular and always busy, and the display of stunning cakes draws in many visitors, including pupils from nearby Marlborough College.

What to see:

The history of Marlborough stretches back centuries. It is even believed that Merlin is buried at Castle Mound – part of Marlborough College. The High Street is mainly Georgian, but older half-timbered houses can be found in the back lanes.

First deserve and then desire.

Stones

High Street, Avebury
Telephone: (01672) 539514

In a former stable block by the ancient stone circles, is this wonderfully rustic, self-service establishment. It is a good place to eat. It is unpretentious and above all concerned with quality. On warm days there is endless space outside in which to enjoy tea.

What to see:

Avebury is a charming place. The village is almost part of the unique circle of standing stones. Though larger than Stonehenge, it has never had the same appeal, yet is far more accessible and the history as fascinating. It was probably built by the 'Beaker Folk' between 2000 and 1600 BC.

THE TEA:

The counter groans with an abundance of home-made cakes and slices. These include shortbreads, banana bread, scones, and Bakewell tart – the list is endless. There are several choices of tea. Price: from £3.50.

OPEN:

Easter to the end of October: Monday to Sunday 10.00am to 6.00pm.

GETTING THERE:

Avebury is on the A4361 (A4) road. Nearest motorway M4. Village car park.

Whose bread I eat his song I sing.

Wiltshire Kitchen

St John's Street, Devizes
Telephone: (01380) 724840

This is a popular, informal spot, good for restoring yourself with a steaming cup of tea any day of the week. All the food is prepared on the premises, the menu changes daily and the baking is memorable and 'moreish'.

What to see:

The museum, in the town of Devizes, exhibits many of the prehistoric remains found in the nearby Salisbury Plains. The town of Trowbridge has many fine buildings built by descendants of Flemish weavers. Another weavers town is Westbury, near which is one of Wiltshire's many famous white horses, cut through the turf.

THE TEA:

The range of cakes often changes but there are always meringues, fruit and chocolate roulades and cream gateaux, as well as cheese scones – served with a variety of teas. Price: from £2.85.

OPEN:

Monday to Saturday 9.00am to 5.30pm. Closed Sunday and Christmas and New Year.

GETTING THERE:

Devizes is on the A361, A360 and A342 roads. Nearest motorway M4. Street parking and town car park.

Deeds are males, words are females.

THE TEA:
Dscover a shop offering bits, bobs and books and unwind in a tea room where food and drink is given due homage with some velvety home baking. Price: from £3.

OPEN:
Daily from 10.30 to 5.30pm, April to end of October. Closed in winter.

GETTING THERE:
Rosedale Abbey is signposted off the A170. Nearest motorway A1(M). Parking in the village.

Never a lip that can't be kissed into smiles.

Abbey Tea Room

Rosedale Abbey
Telephone: (01751) 417475

As the days lengthen and, with luck warm up, thoughts turn once more to "where shall we go for tea?" If you are looking for a perfect corner of England, read on. Rosedale is one such place, for it's full of rich, rolling valleys, brooding green moorland and charming villages sprinkled with white and yellow cottages-one of which is the Abbey Tea Room.

What to see:
In the area are many more tucked away moorland villages which are well worth seeking out. One such is Hutton Le Hole, with an interesting folk museum-once a refuge for persecuted Quakers. Farndale is the largest dale and known for its miles and miles of wild daffodils that bloom in April. Everywhere is fine walking and driving countryside.

Betty's

1 Parliament Street, Harrogate
Telephone: (01423) 502746

Overlooking Montpellier Gardens, Betty's, founded by a Swiss confectioner in 1919, is renowned throughout the North of England and beyond, for the excellence of its baking. Tea is a special treat, and you will simply be spoilt for choice.

What to see:
With public gardens and good shops, Harrogate was once the leading spa town in the north. It abounds in entertainments, fairs and festivals, and makes a good base for touring the surrounding countryside.

THE TEA:
No visitor to Harrogate should miss the experience of Betty's. Look out for the flavoursome, wholemeal bread and scones, generously filled meringues, wicked chocolate cakes and special rich, moist fruit cakes. A fine range of teas includes Indian, China, fruit and herbal. Prices are very reasonable, from £6.

OPEN:
Daily 9.00am to 9.00pm. Closed Christmas day, Boxing day and New Year's day.

GETTING THERE:
Harrogate is on the A61 north of Leeds, and on the A59 west of York. Street parking and pay and display.

Keep your shop and your shop will keep you.

Bolton Abbey Tea Cottage

Bolton Abbey, near Skipton
Telephone: (01756) 710495

Friendly service in a delightfully old-fashioned setting is the recipe for success at this well known tea room. Tea is particularly pleasant in the warmer months sitting in the pretty garden taking in the splendid view. This is truly a place to linger.

What to see:
The lovely wooded banks of the Wharfe stretching north of the priory are well worth exploring. A footbridge and stepping stones cross from the ruins to the east bank, with its pretty views, where tracks and paths can be walked up to Barden Bridge. Inevitably it is a favourite spot with visitors.

THE TEA:
An excellent array of home-made scones, cakes and biscuits are on display it isn't easy making a choice. A selection of tea blends is available, served in china pots by the friendly staff. Prices are very reasonable.

OPEN:
Summer: daily 9.30am to 5.30pm. Winter: closed weekdays November until the end of March.

GETTING THERE:
Bolton Abbey is east of Skipton on the B6160. Car park in the village.

*Too much spoils,
too little does not satisfy.*

Cromwell Eating House

Ripley Castle
Telephone: (0423) 770152

After looking around the castle and gardens, a visit to the tea rooms is a must – particularly if you love chocolate. Fashioned from the old kiln and potter's shop in the stable yard, the tea rooms cater for thousands of visitors every year – yet everything is made on the premises.

What to see:
The castle's fascinating Old Tower, built in 1555, contains much of the family's historic collection. Both James I and Cromwell stayed here. Please check opening times.

*The castle hath a pleasant seat;
the air nimbly and sweetly recommends
itself unto our gentle senses.
– William Shakespeare*

THE TEA:
The most popular items on the menu include, a good variety of cakes, old-fashioned fruit scones and the great wall – a small portion of which will satisfy the sweetest tooth! Tea comes in a homely, earthenware pot. Price: from £3.50.

OPEN:
Easter to the end of October: Monday to Sunday 11.00am to 6.00pm. Phone for other opening times.

GETTING THERE:
Ripley is north of Harrogate on the A61 and A6165 roads. Parking in the castle grounds.

151

philip   collins   ltd

Ms P R Cress

Dear Patricia,

My apologies for the delay in responding to your letter of December 1, 1994.
Phil is out of the country on vacation and I am therefore replying on his behalf.
Phil does prefer tea to coffee and he has a special tea that he drinks before
and during his shows and when he's recording, as he finds it very good for his
throat. I'm including the recipe below in case you are interested.

"Take a large pinch of loose Peppermint tea, a large pinch of Comfrey tea and
a small pinch of Gold Seal tea (or similar). Place all in a tea-pot and add boiling
water. Meanwhile, in a thermos flask, squeeze the juice of half a lemon and
add approximately two teaspoons of honey (depending on your taste). Add
liberal pinch of Cayenne pepper (he use's a lot!). When the tea is brewed -
allowing normal time - pour into flask, shake well and drink."

I'm sorry I can't be of any more help than this. Good luck with the book.

Yours sincerely,

Phil Collins

Annie Callingham (Mrs)
PA to Phil Collins

Duncombe Park

The Tea Room nr Helmsley
Telephone: (01439) 770213

Duncombe House, set in beautiful grounds with sweeping lawns and classical temples, is a friendly 18th-century house full of interesting things to look at. And after in what was the gamekeeper's lodge there is tea. It's got all the modern amenities but also with the warm feeling that only old wood and a glowing fire can engender.
What to see:
For decades the house had been used as a girls school, but after painstaking restoration, it is once again open to the public. Please check opening times. The town of Helmsley has enough to see and do without seeming too touristy. The atmospheric ruins of Rievaulx, the remains of a magnificent abbey are close by and must be seen – but are best visited in low season.

THE TEA:
The food here is country fresh using the very best of local produce. There are always familiar treats such as Yorkshire Parkin or rich fruit cake but soups, quiches and salads also appear on the menu. Go for one of the choice varieties of tea. Price: from £3.95.

OPEN:
Wednesday to Sunday 11.00am to 5.00pm from April to October. July, August, September open daily. Closed in winter.

GETTING THERE:
Duncombe House is signposted off the A170 Pickering to Thirsk road. Nearest motorways M1 M62. Own car park.

Tomorrow is another day.

Magpie Café

14 Pier Road, Whitby
Telephone: (01947) 602058

Take a walk through the town of Whitby and you will come across this popular café, an attractive black and white building overlooking the bustling town's busy harbour. Founded over twenty years ago it is still run by the same family.
What to see:
Whitby is a colourful fishing port and seaside resort which has strong associations with Captain Cook. He served his apprenticeship in a house in Grape Lane and his ships were built here. The local museum contains some of Captain Cook's personal papers as well as a fine fossil collection.

*Well to work and make a fire,
it does care and skill require.*

THE TEA:
A wide range of salads (including seafoods) and light snacks are on the menu, together with a selection of home-made puddings and cakes such as sticky toffee pudding and marzipan and cherry cake. Herbal and fruit teas are served, as well as Indian and China blends. Price: from £4.

OPEN:
Monday to Thursday and Sunday 11.30am to 6.30pm. Friday and Saturday late closing. Closed January.

GETTING THERE:
Whitby is on the A171, A174 and A169 roads. Town car parks.

THE TEA:
There is an appetising selection of home-made cakes, slices and scones. A range of teas includes Indian, China and herbal. Price: from £2.50.

OPEN:
Monday to Sunday 10.00am to 5.00pm. Closed Sundays in November and January to beginning of March.

GETTING THERE:
Pickering is on the A169 and A170 roads. Parking in the town.

Names and nature do often agree.

Mulberries

Bridge Street, Pickering
Telephone: (01751) 472337

After a walk around the town, stop for tea at the charmingly restored Mulberries. The baking is satisfying and the service friendly. If the sun is shining take a table in the peaceful garden, and while away an hour or two!

What to see:
Well worth seeking out in the town of Pickering are: the Beck Isle Museum of Rural Life, the church with early wall paintings, and the ruins of the medieval castle. It makes a good centre for touring the North York Moors and the Vale of Pickering. The North Yorkshire Moors Railway runs from here, and there is an information centre in the station.

THE TEA:
The menu starts with morning choices, runs through lunch and then nibbles on to tea. All the baking is handled with great care. Scones are tender and cakes and puddings are hearty with robust flavours. Price: from £3.

OPEN:
Daily from 10.00am to 10.00pm, End of February to Christmas.

GETTING THERE:
Lealholm is signposted off the A171. Nearest motorway A1(M). Parking in the village.

The new love drives out the old love.

Shepherd's Hall Tea Rooms

Lealholm
Telephone: (01947) 897361

Over a hundred years ago a lovely Victorian house was constructed. Known as the meeting place for the Ancient Order of Shepherds, it was a stop-off for comfort and comradeship. A century on the house has retained those same characteristics, of which the shepherds would be proud, but in the guise of a great little tea room.

What to see:
The North York Moors are one of England's finest national parks-whether walking or driving. The walks and routes are well marked and signposted. In East Yorkshire Castle Howard is a truly magnificent building, begun in 1702 by Vanbrugh and continued while he was working on Blenheim Palace. It houses a wealth of treasures in magnificent rooms and the grounds complete the splendour.

Stonehouse Bakery & Tea Shop

Danby
Telephone: (01287) 660006

Take an old farmhouse, a couple of dedicated bakers and word soon gets around. It is not a pretentious place. If you want to take tea in the lap of luxury, Stonehouse is not for you. But if you like small, unbothersome, well-run places where you can, almost, put your feet up, this is for you.

What to see:

The Dales themselves, with their many interesting features and great natural beauty, are what attract most visitors to the area. Swaledale is the northernmost of all, the most traditional, looking now as it has done for centuries and one of the least visited. The town of Richmond, dominated by the ruins of its castle, deserves a lingering visit.

THE TEA:
All the breads are made with untreated flour and no animal fats are used. Cakes and slices are soft and melting and flavoursome snacks and savouries are also served. Many visitors return again and again for one of the afternoon teas. Price: from £3.

OPEN:
Monday to Saturday from 9.00am to 5.30pm. Closed Sunday.

GETTING THERE:
Danby is signposted off the A171 Whitby road. Parking in the village.

A kind heart loseth nought at last.

Swinsty Tea Garden

Fewston House, Fewston
Telephone: (01943) 880 637

Here, overlooking a picturesque reservoir, you'll enjoy some enterprising home-cooking. Only organic flour is used for the baking, while most of the vegetables come from the country herb garden. Altogether a delightful find.

What to see:

A number of Yorkshire's most historic towns and villages are within easy reach. West of Ripon are the spectacular ruins of Fountains Abbey – founded in the 12th century by Archbishop Thurston and monks of the Cistercian order. The ruins give a comprehensive picture of life in a medieval monastery.

THE TEA:
The menu offers a simple but extremely enjoyable selection of scones and just-baked cakes. There is a choice of teas including fruit and herbal. Price: from £3. No cream used.

OPEN:
Saturday and Sunday 11.00am to 5.00pm. Closed Monday to Friday

GETTING THERE:
Fewston is seven miles west of Harrogate on the A59 Nearest motorway M1 Own car park

A garden is a lovesome thing.
T E Brown

155

Taylor's Tea Rooms

46 Stonegate, York
Telephone: (0904) 622865

Because of its location – not far from the Minster – this is one of York's best known tea rooms. Downstairs the aromas of exotic teas and coffees tempt one to buy by the sackful! Upstairs the tea room is welcoming and refreshing.

What to see:
Medieval York is very well preserved, the narrow streets of Stonegate and The Shambles being two of the best examples. But the Minster, built between 1220 and 1472, the largest British medieval cathedral, is the city's main glory. It contains magnificent stained glass windows, the Five Sisters and the East Window being the best known.

THE TEA:
In the afternoon the cake trolley carries traditional Yorkshire tarts, fruit cakes and cream confections. And, of course there is a marvellous selection of teas. Price: from £4.

OPEN:
Monday to Sunday 9.00am to 5.30pm. Closed over the Christmas holiday and New Year's day.

GETTING THERE:
York can be approached on the following main roads: A19, A59, A64, A166 and the A1079. Parking in the city car parks.

Kindness is the noblest weapon to conquer with.

Yorkshire (West)

Ashwood

The Old Hall, Church Lane, Esholt
Telephone: (01274) 597866

A delightful old stone building in a really rustic setting, stands in the village where the 'Emmerdale Farm' series is filmed. The walls are adorned with photographs of the actors and actresses, and souvenirs are on sale. On warm days arrive early and enjoy tea in the garden.

What to see:
Not much further afield are Haworth (the Brontë's home), the beautiful Worth Valley, the village of Holmfirth where 'Last of the Summer Wine' is filmed for television, and the city of Bradford, with its outstanding National Photographic Museum. There's plenty to do and see in this part of Yorkshire.

THE TEA:
The tea room offers freshly made sandwiches, scones and tempting home-made cakes, served with a choice of teas. Price: from £2.

OPEN:
April to October: Monday to Sunday 10.00am to 6.00pm. Winter: Sunday only.

GETTING THERE:
Esholt is north of Bradford on the A658. Nearest Motorways M1 and M62. Parking in the village.

Yorkshire born and Yorkshire bred.

Cobbled Way

60 Main Street, Haworth
Telephone: (01535) 642735

The village of Haworth is all grey-stone houses and slate roofs and is about the same size as it was when the Brontë's lived there. After climbing the steep, cobbled main street it is a relief to find a pretty little tea room offering good home-baking.
What to see:
The Parsonage where the Brontë's lived is now an evocative museum. Inside, the rooms are furnished with family articles including the sofa on which Emily died, Charlotte's work box, and the minute books that the children wrote in secret. Beyond the graveyard are glimpses of the desolate moors. It is a place that thrills some visitors and depresses others.

THE TEA:
The menu offers a wide range of sandwiches and snacks but, scones and cakes are the ultimate temptation served with a choice of freshly made teas. Price: from £2.50.

OPEN:
Monday to Sunday 10.30am to 5.30pm or so.

GETTING THERE:
Haworth is on the A6033 road. Nearerst motorways M62 and M65. Village car park.

Humble hearts have humble desires.

Wrinkled Stocking Tea Room

Huddersfield Road, Holmfirth
Telephone: (01484) 681408

The BBC TV series 'Last of the Summer Wine' was filmed in Holmfirth, and this welcoming tea room stands next to Nora Batty's cottage (hence the unusual name). The walls are adorned with photographs and cartoons of the series' stars.
What to see:
Holmfirth has become a tourist centre made famous by the TV series, and can become very crowded. The area around here is not only scenic but full of moorland walks, nature trails and stately homes to visit. The town of Huddersfield is a short drive away.

*Show me that I'm everywhere
And get me home for tea.
George Harrison*

THE TEA:
You can enjoy sandwiches cut to order, fruit pies, chocolate cakes, tasty scones as well as two set teas. There is a fine selection of tea blends. Price: from £2.25.

OPEN:
Daily 10.00am to 5.30pm. Winter earlier closing.

GETTING THERE:
Holmfirth is south of Huddersfield on the A635 and A6023 roads. Nearest motorways M1, M62 and M63. Village car park.

Abbotsford House

Melrose
Telephone: (01896) 75 2043

Abbotsford, set on the River Tweed, was the home of Sir Walter Scott from 1812-1832. It contains numerous historical and personal relics, a fine collection of arms, a library with more than 9,000 rare books and Scott's study, still much as he left it. Overlooking the garden is the tea room.

What to see:
Further connections with Sir Walter Scott can be made at the ruins of Melrose Abbey, thought of as Scotland's finest ruined abbey. It was frequently ravaged by the English, but the beauty of it can still be seen. The heart of Robert the Bruce is said to have been buried beneath the East window. The museum tells the story of the abbey.

Abbey Cottage

Main Street, New Abbey
Telephone: (01387) 850377

It is worth a detour, to visit this charming, little tea room with a craft shop attached. Visitors will enjoy the hearty home-baking, and friendly, warm service. The garden overlooks the ruins of Sweetheart Abbey, altogether a most romantic spot.

What to see:
Sweetheart Abbey, founded in 1273 by Devorgill, Lady of Galloway is so called because she decreed that her husband's heart should be buried with her before the High Altar. Dumfries is an interesting town and the place where Robbie Burns ended his days. His house is now a museum, and he is buried in St Michael's church.

THE TEA:
The place ticks with a no-nonsense approach to food. For cake lovers, and there are many of us, scones, shortbreads, sponges and biscuits are all baked carefully. Light snacks and sandwiches are readily prepared. Price: from £3.

OPEN:
Monday to Saturday from 10.00am to 5.00pm. Sunday from 2-5.00pm. Easter to mid-October only. There is an entrance fee.

GETTING THERE:
Abbotsford is signposted off the A7 road. Own car park.

---

*Only one good:
Knowledge.*

THE TEA:
You can sample home-made date slice, walnut cake and caramel shortbread, scones are served with fresh preserve and cream and there is a choice of teas. Price: from £2.

OPEN:
Easter to October: Monday to Sunday 10.00am to 5.00pm. Closed November to Easter.

GETTING THERE:
New Abbey is south of Dumfries on the A710. Nearest motorway M6. Car park in the village.

The joy of the heart makes the face fair.

Black's Tea Rooms

144 Argyll Street, Dunoon
Telephone: (01369) 2311

This charming combination of a bakery and tea room allows you to taste all the flavoursome cakes and crusty breads, and take them home too. So people come, they visit, and they chat as they wait for their tea and cakes.
Price: from £2.
What to see:
Dunoon is a popular and lively resort and makes a good centre for touring this region of Scotland as there are numerous ferry and steamer trips during the season. Not far away are Holy Loch, the famous nuclear submarine base, and Benmore House noted for its botanic gardens and open to the public. Please check opening times.

THE TEA:
The menu here aspires to offer simple, unfussy cakes, scones and pastries made with the highest-quality ingredients. Several blends of tea are readily available.
Price: from £2.

OPEN:
Monday to Saturday 9.00am to 5.00pm. Closed Sunday, Bank Holidays and Christmas and New Year.

GETTING THERE:
Dunoon is on the A815. Nearest motorway M8. Take the ferry from Gourock. Parking in the town car parks.

Better at home than a mile from it.

Brambles

College Street, St Andrews
Telephone: (01334) 475380

Situated in the centre of St Andrews, Brambles is housed in a characterful old building. Adding to the atmosphere is an interesting mix of visitors from university students to Americans touring Scotland.
What to see:
St Andrews is an entrancing place to visit, with numerous claims to fame. It's University is the oldest in Scotland, its ruined cathedral was once the largest in the country. In the ancient ruined Castle the 'bottle dungeons' can still be seen. It also contains charming Georgian streets, and golden sands stretching into a blue (but cold) sea.

THE TEA:
There are hot snacks and sandwiches but the home-made cakes are the outstanding temptation. There is a choice of teas. Brambles is self service.
Price: from £3.

OPEN:
April to October, Monday to Saturday and Bank Holidays 9.00am to 5.00pm. Sunday 12 noon to 5.00pm. Phone for winter openings.

GETTING THERE:
St Andrews is south of Dundee on the A91, A915 and A917 roads. Nearest motorway M90. Parking in the town car parks.

Temperance is the best physic.

THE TEA:

The set afternoon tea brings finger sandwiches and excellent scones served with jam and cream, plus a choice of well prepared cakes and pastries. The selection of teas includes Indian, China, fruit and herbal. Price: set tea from £9.50.

OPEN:

Daily 3.00 to 5.30pm. Throughout the year.

GETTING THERE:

On the city's main street, near the railway station and castle. Restricted parking in the main city area.

What one relishes, nourishes.

The Caledonian Hotel

Princes Street, Edinburgh
Telephone: (0131) 225 2433

Centrally located on historic Princes Street in the heart of the city, The Caledonian is one of Scotland's grandest hotels. A full afternoon tea is served in the supremely gracious surroundings of the traditional-style lounge.

What to see:

The state apartments at Edinburgh Castle contain the Scottish Crown Jewels. The Palace of Holyrood House is the official Scottish residence of the Queen. It contains relics of Mary, Queen of Scots, fine furniture and paintings. The annual Edinburgh Festival, one of the largest arts festivals in the world, attracts thousands of visitors.

THE TEA:

You won't leave for the journey home remotely hungry and you may even have bid for a jug and bowl as a reminder of a well spent afternoon. The cakes, scones and biscuits are cracking
Price: set tea from £3.

OPEN:

Daily from 9.30am to 5.30pm- Tuesday closed. Wednesday to Saturday also open evenings 7.30-9.30pm from Easter to end of September. Open in winter, but please phone for days and times.

GETTING THERE:

Newcastleton is on the B6357 road. Nearest motorway M6. Parking in the town.

Copshaw Kitchen

Newcastleton
Telephone: (013873) 75250

Most of us will turn the old jalopy round and chug a fair old distance in search of excellent food, it is an added joy when the final destination turns out to be good fun as well. To begin with, the name is a little misleading. Copshaw isn't the tea room, Holm Fayre is, but you can have tea in both and in the parlour as well! And if that isn't enough the place is chock-a-block with antiques.

What to see:

The history of the area is everywhere illustrated by the buildings and ruins. At Hermitage is the restored but daunting Hermitage Castle, the scene of many grim events. Mary Queen of Scots visited in 1566, and nearly died of a fever after riding the forty miles to Jedburgh and back to see Bothwell.

Knowledge is a treasure, but practice the key.

Green Shutter Tea Room

28 Bath Street, Largs
Telephone: (01475) 672252

This popular modern tea room is right on the seafront with lovely views across the Clyde estuary to the Isle of Bute. There is a jolly, friendly atmosphere with helpful service – even when it gets busy!

What to see:
Largs is a most attractive seaside resort with a fine beach. There are ferry services from Largs to The Cumbraes, two small islands off the Ayrshire coast. There are car and passenger ferries to Bute from Wemyss Bay and Colintraive. Rothesay the former capital of Bute is full of interest.

THE TEA:
In the afternoon cake stands appear laden with shortbread, meringues, cream cakes and fruit slices, served with a choice of tea blends. Price: from £3.

OPEN:
March to October: Monday to Sunday 10.00am to 6.00pm. Closed November to the end of February.

GETTING THERE:
Largs is on the A78 A760 roads. Nearest motorway M8. Parking on the seafront.

A Scottish mist will wet an Englishman to the skin.

The Jenny Traditional Tea Rooms

Royal Exchange Square, Glasgow
Telephone: (0141) 204 4988

The Jenny is a serene retreat. It evokes the atmosphere of a Victorian tea-room-cum-coffee-house for which Glasgow was once as famous as Vienna. The decor is cottage style and waitresses dressed in floral prints add to the charm. It's good either to come with friends, or to wind down on your own.

What to see:
For such a large city, Glasgow is lacking in major historical sights but still offers the visitor a lively and stimulating visit. There are galleries to peruse, smart shops to visit and flea markets to rummage in. The cathedral and Provan's Lordship, the oldest house in the city, are of interest. Loch Lomond is a lovely place to visit and virtually on Glasgow's doorstep.

THE TEA:
Home-made cakes and biscuits ooze with flavour as does all the cooking. The Jenny serves a hearty breakfast, filling lunches and, of course, set afternoon teas. Price: from £3.

OPEN:
Monday to Saturday from 8.00am to 7.00pm. Sundays from 11-7.00pm. Also opens on 3 evenings for traditional Scottish dinners. Please phone.

GETTING THERE:
Glasgow is on the A77 A88 A83 roads. Nearest motorways M8 M73 M74. Car Parks.

Disperse the clouds and mist and there is the blue sky.

Dear Patricia,

thanx for your recent letter with regard to tea.

It has to be an absolute favourite of mine. I'm similar to you, in that my teapot's never empty and there's nothing better than Betty's in Harrogate to take a friend for our very traditional English tea.

Not only that, a cuppa really wakes me up and is essential to get my voice going when I'm working. Also, no gossip is complete without tea & biscuits!

Good luck with your book & cheers!

Kind regards,

Su Pollard

162

Kailzie Gardens

Kailzie, Peebles
Telephone: (01721) 722807

It's a difficult decision to make. Does one visit Kailzie on a glorious summer day or, on an a golden, autumnal day that only Scotland can produce? Whatever, the place buzzes with visitors attracted by the scenery, the superb gardens and the art gallery. But the added bonus is the good food served in what was the Old Coach House and stables.

What to see:

Peebles is a busy shopping centre, well known for its tweed mills and makes a good centre for touring the surrounding area. Beautifully situated on the River Tweed, is one of the most striking of the Border castles, Neidpath, originally 13th century and lived in continuously since then. Please check opening times.

THE TEA:
A proper afternoon tea featuring sandwiches, cakes and scones is included in the menu, but cooked lunches, light meals and wholesome baked minimarvels are also available. Price: from £3.50.

OPEN:
Daily from 11.00am to 5.30pm- March to October only. Also some Saturday evenings. Please check.

GETTING THERE:
Kailzie is on the B7062 roads. Nearest motorways M6 M74. Own car park.

History repeats itself.

Kind Kyttock's Kitchen

Cross Wynd, Falkland
Telephone: (01337) 857477

The unusual name refers to a kindly woman, Kind Kyttock. Long ago she served food and drink to weary travellers passing through the area. This tradition of hospitality continues, at this pleasing tea room, to this very day.

What to see:

Falkland Place, was built by James IV and James V in the 16th century, and has connections with Mary Queen of Scots. It is well worth a visit, the gardens are particularly fine and the tennis court is one of the oldest in Britain. Charles II created the Scots Guards here in 1650. Please check opening times.

A contented mind is a continual feast.

THE TEA:
There is a wide range of home-made cakes, slices and shortbreads. Don't leave without trying an afternoon tea of Scotch pancakes served with a pot of loose leaf tea – delicious! Price: from £3.

OPEN:
Tuesday to Sunday 10.30am to 5.30pm. Closed Monday, Christmas and 2 weeks in January.

GETTING THERE:
Falkland is on the A912. Nearest motorway M90. Street parking and car parks.

Old School Tea Rooms

Ringford
Telephone: (0155 722) 250

An old, three roomed schoolhouse has been converted to create this unusual tea room. There are echoes of the past in the blackboard and in the handbell that summons service. Old school photographs line the walls and the partition that once separated two classrooms now divides the tea room from the craft shop.

What to see:
Ringford is a good centre for exploring the surrounding countryside and a number of historic towns in the area. Kirkcudbright to name but one, has streets unchanged since the 18th century, interesting buildings and the imposing MacLellan's Castle, built in 1582.

THE TEA:
Refreshments offered are a far cry from school dinners and include, freshly made sandwiches, home-baked cakes and scones, with a choice of teas. Price: from £2.

OPEN:
Monday to Sunday 10.00am to 5.00pm during the summer months. Days and hours vary in winter.

GETTING THERE:
Ringford is between Castle Douglas and Kirkcudbright on the A75 and A762. Nearest motorway M6. Ample parking.

Talking comes by nature, silence by understanding.

Argyll Tea Room

Argyll Street, Oban
Telephone: (01631) 66945

Timber-lined walls and a simple beamed ceiling give a homely aspect to this small, family-run tea room tucked away in a side street just steps away from the waterfront. Popular with both local residents and visitors for the excellence of its home baking, it offers some very tasty snacks and cakes.

What to see:
Centre of a network of boat services linking the islands with the mainland, plenty of comings and goings make it a fascinating spot. The ivy-clad keep of Dunollie Castle stands above Loch Linnhe. The cathedral built in 1932 was designed by Sir Giles Scott. The whole area is fascinating with rugged and beautiful scenery.

THE TEA:
They love baking here, so look out for scones, pancakes, tea breads, macaroon tarts and a variety of cakes. There is a limited selection of teas. Price: from £2.

OPEN:
Monday to Saturday from 10.00am to 5.00pm. Closed Sunday. Open during winter months best to check.

GETTING THERE:
Oban is approached on the A85 A816 roads. Parking in the town.

A tale never loses in the telling.

Stables, Queen's Court

41 Sandgate, Ayr
Telephone: (01292) 283704

The stables, in a pleasant, restored 18th-century courtyard, filled with plants and flowers, is popular with town residents and visitors alike. The menu here is refreshingly local, and includes some excellent baking.

What to see:

Ayr is an ancient town with much of historical interest. However, visitors come from all over the world to follow the Burns Heritage trail, which includes the thatched cottage at Alloway where he was born, the Brig o'Doon, (13th-century bridge) where Tam o'Shanter escaped the evil witches, and much else besides. Best visited out of high season.

THE TEA:

On the tea menu there are, fresh baked scones, cakes, and oatcakes, a Scottish speciality delicious when served warm. There is a small selection of teas. Price: from £2.50.

OPEN:

Monday to Saturday 10.00am to 5.00pm. Sunday 1.00 to 5.00pm summer only.

GETTING THERE:

Ayr is on the A70 and A77 roads. Nearest motorway M74. Car parks in the town.

Painters and poets have leave to lie.

1745 Cottage Tea Room, Traquair House

Traquair House, Innerleithen
Telephone: (01896) 830323

Traquair House is one of Scotland's oldest and most romantic inhabited mansions. Though most of the present buildings date from the 17th century few other places have so much to offer in terms of ambience, history and natural beauty. You get the feeling that every nook and cranny, every brick and stone could whisper secrets.

What to see:

The Borders scenery is majestic without being too austere, and pleasantly varied, while there are no end of romantic abbey ruins, ancient castles and small, friendly towns to visit. The hills offer the walker, and driver, miles of secluded glens – and a refreshing quiet not easily found nowadays.

THE TEA:

Afterwards make a point of visiting the Cottage Tea Room to sample some edible treasures. Main dishes and snacks are comforting and scones, flapjacks and fruit slices are the ultimate treat. Price: from £4.

OPEN:

Easter week, 12.30 to 5.30pm daily, then from 1 May to end of September. July and August open from 10.30am. Entrance fees to house and garden.

GETTING THERE:

The House is on the B709, south of Innerleithen. Own car park.

Let the piper call the tune.

Willow Tea Room

217 Sauchiehall Street, Glasgow
Telephone: (0141) 332 0521

No visit to Glasgow is complete without a visit to the Willow Tea Rooms. It has been carefully restored to the original design of architect Charles Rennie Mackintosh and is filled with reproductions of his stylish Art Nouveau furniture.

What to see:

Glasgow is a cheerful, lively place. It has historical buildings, many parks, good theatres, a fine cathedral and the River Clyde. Within an hour's drive, you can be in Edinburgh, the Highlands, or by the banks of Loch Lomond. The Clyde flows through Glasgow, and one of the most enjoyable things to do is to sail down the river from Anderston Quay.

THE TEA:

Scones, cakes and pastries are served as well as a set afternoon tea. There is a choice of Indian, China and herbal teas. Waitress service. Price: from £3.50.

OPEN:

Monday to Saturday 9.30am to 4.30pm. Closed Sunday.

GETTING THERE:

Glasgow is on the A77, A80 and A82 roads. Nearest motorways M8, M73 and M74. Meter parking and town car parks.

The time to come is no more ours than the time past.

Wales

Afonwen Craft & Antique Centre

Afonwen, near Mold
Telephone: (01352) 720965

Have you ever suddenly realised that you are in the right place at the right time? Because that, is the situation in which you will find yourself when visiting the old mill. Back in 1786 this historic building produced paper for the Bank of England. Today, with all its original features retained, the old mill has become a centre for cuppas, crafts and antiques.

What to see:

Denbigh is a busy little town overlooking the Vale of Clwyd. Perched above it is a ruined castle with a trio of towers and a notable arch; the figure on the summit is believed to represent Edward I. The whole area is criss-crossed with scenic drives.

THE TEA:

Happy hours can be spent here sampling anything from a three course lunch to an impressive afternoon tea. Smiling, motherly waitresses dressed in white pinnies will take your order. Price: from £3.50.

OPEN:

All year, Tuesday to Sunday from 9.30am to 5.30pm. Closed Mondays except Bank Holidays.

GETTING THERE:

Afonwen is on the A541, Mold-Denbigh road. Nearest motorways M6 M56. Own car park.

She had rather kiss than spin.

Bank Cottage Tea Rooms

The Bank, Newtown
Telephone: (01686) 625771

Once in a blue moon it is good todip a spoon in the maelstrom we call life! Don't take that to mean a couple of days in the Casbah. A weekend in Wales can be just as wicked. If you chance upon Bank Cottage, the epitome of tea tranquillity and comfort, then heaven has been sampled.

What to see:
The main interest for many visitors will be that Robert Owen, the Socialist reformer, was born here in 1771. He devoted his life to trying to improve conditions in the factories. He founded nurseries, set up his own mill and in old age returned to Newtown and is buried in the churchyard. A drive south along the A483 offers enchanting mountain scenery.

THE TEA:
All is tickety-boo. At tea time choose from plain or wholemeal scones, glistening, fruit crumbles, terrific cheesecakes and plenty of other indulgences. Price: from £2.50.

OPEN:
Monday to Saturday from 9.00am to 5.00pm. All year round. Closed Sunday.

GETTING THERE:
Newtown is on the A483 A489 roads. Parking in the town.

Those who thirst for knowledge always get it.

Bumble

Charles Street, Wrexham
Telephone: (01978) 355023

A good place to start your wanderings in Wrexham is at Bumble. It offers a hotch-potch of good things at your fingertips, and whether you're looking for a teacup, entire place setting or a flamboyant suit, they can all wait as you allow the long day to turn in to afternoon, as the poet put it.

What to see:
One of the attraction for visitors to Wrexham is the 15th-century church of St Giles; the other is a 17th-century house detailing life 'upstairs' and 'downstairs.' Shrewsbury, Chester and all of North Wales are within driving distance, through scenic areas. Whilst nearby Llangollen is home to the international Eisteddfod held annually in July.

Honours change manners.

THE TEA:
Tea is a hearty event, with steaming pots of the leaf and crumbly teacakes ready for butter and jam. If you're lucky plates of meringues, cheesecakes and sultana scones will make an appearance. Light lunches and specials are always available. Price: from £3

OPEN:
Monday to Saturday from 9.00am to 5.00pm. Closed Sundays and Bank Holidays.

GETTING THERE:
Wrexham is on the A483, A525 A534 roads. Nearest motorway M6. Parking in the town.

THE TEA:
The cakes, of the how-temptingly-displayed-I-am-variety, are really good. The scones are flaky and come with quantities of Caldy cream and a sprightly list of teas.
Price: from £3.

OPEN:
Daily, all year round from 10.00am to 6.00pm. 5.30pm in winter.

GETTING THERE:
Tenby is on the A477, A478 roads. Nearest motorway M4. Restricted parking in the town.

The world is a long journey.

Celtic Fare Tea Rooms

St Julian's Street, Tenby
Telephone: (01834) 845258

Even if your mother or father never baked a cake in their lives, the food here will have you dreaming that you're eating in someone's home. The considerable charm. This is further increased by the miscellany of jugs and teapots hanging from the beams and the fire lighting up the hearth.

What to see:

This is the best known resort in the county, with a harbour, sandy beaches and a fine golf course. The town castle and walls date from the 13th century but many of the buildings are Georgian. Tenby offers all the pleasures of a traditional seaside holiday. There are boat trips to Caldy Island.

THE TEA:
Fill your plate with wholesome Welsh food as everyone imagines it, made with the minimum of fuss or frills from honest ingredients. Special delights are Welsh cakes, banana bread and Bara Brith.
Price: from £2.50.

OPEN:
Monday to Saturday from 10.00am to 5.30pm. Closed Sunday.

GETTING THERE:
Builth Wells is on the A470 A483 roads. Nearest motorway M5. Parking in the town.

Cosy Corner Tea Room

High Street, Builth Wells
Telephone: (01982) 553585

Old stone, character and history make a strong appeal to first-timers at this tea room where good baking and local specialities are also very important. Inside, wooden tables, pretty curtains and lots of pictures give the place an easy relaxing warmth. Loyal customers think nothing of travelling miles to take tea here.

What to see:

It is outdoor activities which bring most people here. There is wonderful walking country. Forest trails are well marked and there are plenty of guided walks too. For the true adventurer, hang-gliding, climbing, caving and water sports await.

She that will kiss will do worse.

The Drover's Rest Tea Rooms

The Square, Llanwrtyd Wells
Telephone: (01591) 610264

It was drizzling. The family, never mind the natives, was restless. The only solution was to find somewhere quickly for a spot of tucker. And that's how The Drover's Rest was chanced upon. The place has been welcoming travellers, with courtesy, good food and a smile, for years-and long may it continue to do so.

What to see:
On the strength of its sulphur springs, Llanwrtyd Wells was once a popular spa town. But the fashion for such things having passed it is now a very pleasant holiday resort. It stands in an area of natural beauty, One can drive for miles on deserted roads among hills of heather and bracken and through valleys of velvet green.

THE TEA:
Some very hard decisions to make. Almost every appetite is catered for from gourmet lunches to robust teas. Local recipes have been revived, and many visitors acknowledge a passion for the 'Welsh Tea'. Price: from £3.55.

OPEN:
Daily from 9.30am to 5.00pm. Also open some evenings for dinner. Please check.

GETTING THERE:
Llanwrtyd Wells is on the A483 road. Nearest motorway M5. Parking in the town.

The world is but a little place after all.

Gliffaes Hotel

Crickhowell, Powys
Telephone: (01874) 730371

Gliffaes is a country house hotel high in the Usk Valley, reached via a narrow winding road. The atmosphere is one of friendliness and informality, while great care is taken to maintain the best standards of British cooking.

What to see:
Scenery is the main but not the only attraction of the area. There are plenty of castles to visit including one at nearby Crickhowell; and everywhere one finds good local craft workshops. However, it is the outdoor activities which bring most people here. There is superb walking country and numerous scenic car drives to enjoy.

Love lasts as long as money endures.

THE TEA:
Afternoon tea, served in the lounge, or on the terrace, with its glorious views of the surrounding hills and the River Usk, is a real treat. The hotel is renowned for the quality of its home-made teas. Price: £5.90 a full tea.

OPEN:
Monday to Sunday 3.30 to 5.30pm for tea. Open throughout the year.

GETTING THERE:
The hotel is one mile off the A40 on the B4558. Own car park.

169

Lake Vyrnwy Hotel

Llanwddyn
Telephone: (01691) 870692

If you relish the feeling of discovering somewhere unique and private, then, Lake Vyrnwy hotel is perfect. It is the kind of place that offers space, peace, quiet, and a certain ambience that, quite possibly, nurtures literary and romantic spirits, who knows? Everywhere is old fashioned and personal, worlds away from hotel-motel chains, 'have a nice day' staff and portion control.

What to see:

The lake is the largest in Wales and was formed by damming the River Vyrnwy to make a reservoir for Liverpool. It was completed in 1891 and people came from all over the world to admire it. Although the dam is still an imposing sight, visitors come now for the peace and beauty of the lake. There are superb opportunities for scenic drives, on quiet roads, particularly in low season.

Oaklands

Llanfair Kilgeddin, near Abergavenny
Telephone: (01873) 840218

Oaklands, an easy fifteen minute drive from Abergavenny, is one of those genuine, satisfying family places where the food is home cooked using the best ingredients. Summer is a good time to visit, for then umbrella topped tables decorate the well kept garden of this village house.

What to see:

Nearby Usk is a charming small town, and stands in an area of natural beauty. On the outskirts are the remains of a fine Norman castle and a Benedictine nunnery. It is in an area well known for its fishing.

He that would be well,
needs not go far from his own house.

THE TEA:
The cooking and baking are careful and traditional, and loved because of that. The menu offers freshly made sandwiches, warmed scones and toasted teacakes.
Price: from £5.

OPEN:
All year, Monday to Sunday from 3.00pm for tea.

GETTING THERE:
Llanwddyn is on the B4393. Own car park.

Life is half spent before we know what it is.

THE TEA:
Among the specialities are Welsh cakes with nutmeg, fruit tarts, fudge slices and scones with home-made preserve and clotted cream, served with pots of well made tea.
Price: from £2.50.

OPEN:
Monday to Sunday 1.00 to 5.00pm (or so). Easter to October.

GETTING THERE:
Llanfair Kilgeddin is on the B4598 Usk Abergavenny road. Own car park. (Look for the 'teas' sign).

Ogmore Farm

Ewenny, near Bridgend
Telephone: (01656) 653650

The delightful tiny garden, overlooking the ruins of Ogmore Castle on the banks of the Ewenny River, is ideal for a leisurely afternoon tea. In addition to the garden there is a homely rustic tea room, where farmhouse baking is the speciality, and a warm Welsh welcome the norm!.

What to see:
The castle lies just above the mouth of the Ewenny River at an important ford where the river is still crossed by ancient stepping stones. It was built there by William de Londres in the 12th century.

<hr>

Blue are the faraway hills

<hr>

THE TEA:
The baking here is most agreeable, with a menu that consists of Welsh cakes, fruit tarts and toasted teacakes. And the Bara Brith is a must-served with a well made pot of tea. Price: from £3.

OPEN:
Easter to end of October: Tuesday to Sunday 11.00am to 1.00pm and 3.00 to 6.00pm. Possibility of weekend opening during the winter months. Please check.

GETTING THERE:
Ogmore is one and a half miles upstream from Ogmore-by-Sea on the B4524. Nearest motorway M4. Car park area.

Pinnacle Café

Capel Curig
Telephone: (016904) 201

For hikers, ramblers, old softies, lovers of the Sound of Music, in fact anyone in the area, the Pinnacle is an irresistible magnet. When you need warmth and comfort you'll discover it here. If you've been searching for a woolly hat with a pom-pom, or a long ball of string, you need look no further. All this, plus genial company is the order of the day.

What to see:
This is the heart of Snowdonia, with Caernarvon in one direction and Bangor in the other. For many visitors to the area, the aim is to stand on top of Snowdon and savour the views. There are well trodden paths, a rack-and-pinion railway, and for the experienced climber ropes and crampons to assist you to the summit. British Himalayan climbers often train in the area.

<hr>

Don't cry before you are hurt.

<hr>

THE TEA:
Early birds pop in for breakfast. Light lunches and snacks are also served and a good variety of home-made scones, cakes and pastries are soon scoffed. A sprinkling of teas are just the ticket. Price: from £3.

OPEN:
Monday to Sunday from 7.30am to around 5.30pm.

GETTING THERE:
Capel Curig is on the A5 Bethesda to Betws-y-Coed road. Parking available.

The Plas

High Street, Harlech
Telephone: (01766) 780204

The Plas, Welsh for large house, is not designed for popping in and out of quickly, so set aside a long languid afternoon for savouring the atmosphere. People, from all over the place, wander through to the conservatory or the garden, take tea and stare at the view, or better still into one another's eyes.

What to see:

The castle is one of many built in the 13th century by Edward I to subdue the rebellious Welsh. The town of Harlech offers an eclectic range of attractions besides the castle. Nearby are the Llanfair Slate Caverns, the Royal St David's Golf Course and Portmeirion – the Lleyn peninsula's famous fantasy village. To the north rise the mountains of Snowdonia.

THE TEA:
The menu is simple and satisfying. Care has gone into the choices for light lunches and snacks, and an assortment of cakes, pastries and scones wait to be demolished. Price: from £2.50.

OPEN:
Monday to Sunday from 9.00am to 8.00pm from mid March to Christmas.

GETTING THERE:
Harlech is on the A496. Parking in the town car parks.

Little wealth, little care.

Powis Castle

Welshpool, Powys
Telephone: (01938) 554336

Set in a fine medieval deer park, Powis is among the most romantic of the chain of castles which guarded the Welsh Marches. Here in an historic atmosphere a large but inviting tea room has been created.

What to see:

Powis is a magnificent castle with battlements, terraced gardens – considered the finest in Europe, and acres of parkland. There is a museum devoted to Lord Clive of India which features a glittering array of Indian art and treasures. Welshpool is the terminus of the Welshpool and Llanfair Light Railway. The journey takes you through gentle woodland countryside.

THE TEA:
Visitors to the tea room enjoy home-made scones, generous portions of cake and a choice of teas, all served by efficient staff. Price: from £2.75.

OPEN:
The castle and tea room are open from Easter to November. Please check days and times.

GETTING THERE:
The castle is one mile south of Welshpool on the A483. Nearest motorway M54. Ample car parking.

If it were not for hope, the heart would break.

Plas Glyn-y-Weddw Gallery

The Widows Glen, Llanbedrog
Telephone: (01758) 740763

Plas Glyn-y-Weddw is one of those old-time tried and true, elegant houses that seem to age very well indeed. Now returned to its former glory as a gallery, you can enjoy exhibits of paintings, drawings and sculptures and when the appetite for art has been satisfied cross the hall to the tea room that also glows with an antique charm.

What to see:
The peninsula is one of the most beautiful and varied corners of Wales, offering wild dramatic scenery in one direction, while in the other sheltered bays and safe, sandy beaches. Pwllheli has become a popular resort with modern attractions. In sharp contrast seek out the old part to discover a Georgian arcade and Victorian canopied shops.

THE TEA:
Daily specials use only fresh top-quality ingredients, and the cakes, scones and pastries are of the melt-in-your-mouth variety. This is food of forgotten virtues. Price: from £3.50.

OPEN:
Monday to Sunday from 10.00am to 6.00pm. Easter to the end of October.

GETTING THERE:
Llanbedrog is on the A497 A499 roads. Own car park.

As good love comes as goes.

Sandbach

78a Mustyn Street, LLandudno
Telephone: (01492) 876522

There's old-world charm in abundance in this delightful tea room, situated on the first floor of a shop selling hand-made chocolates and sweets. The craft rooms display prints, cards and hand-made glass, so enjoy a browse after tea.

What to see:
Llandudno is a very pleasant seaside resort with a pier, good shops, galleries and a museum. At the top of the Great Orme headland is the small church of St Tudno. At the summit you can take the cabin lift or the Victorian tramway, the longest cable-car system in Britain.

The best things come in small packages.

THE TEA:
A selection of biscuits, cakes and pastries is served from the trolley, and the Welsh cream tea is a must. There is an excellent range of teas. Price: from £3.50.

OPEN:
Monday to Saturday 9.30am to 5.30pm. Closed Sunday, Christmas and New Year.

GETTING THERE:
Llandudno is on the A55. Nearest motorways M53 and M56. Street parking and town car parks.

THE TEA:
All aboard for well brewed cups of tea and some homely baking: rock cakes, apple and almond slices and fruit scones to name but three. Friendly counter service. Price: from £1.50.

OPEN:
April to 31 October: Monday to Sunday 10.30am to 5.30pm. Closed November to end of March.

GETTING THERE:
Tintern is on the A466. The station is just passed the village on the Monmouth road. Own car park.

Much travelling teaches how to see.

THE TEA:
At teatime guests are invited to enjoy home-made scones, Bara Brith, buttery biscuits and cream sponges, served with a choice of tea blends. Price: from £2.

OPEN:
Easter to end of November: Tuesday to Sunday 10.30am to 5.30pm. Closed Monday but open Bank Holidays.

GETTING THERE:
Llanrwst is on the A470 and A548 roads. Car park available.

Tintern Station

Tintern, Gwent
Telephone: (01291) 689566

This unusual stop for tea is in the former British Rail station at Tintern. Visitors can choose to sit inside the old, carefully restored waiting room, while outside there is a large picnic area with views of gently sloping hills, with grazing sheep. The signal box is now filled with local crafts and two old carriages house displays and local tourist information.

What to see:
Dating from the 12th century Tintern Abbey is one of the most beautiful and extensive of Cistercian ruins to be found in Britain. An exhibition illustrates the history of the abbey and also the Wye Valley.

Tu Hwnt I'r Bont

Llanrwst, Gwynedd.
Telephone: (01492) 640138

Close to the bridge that spans the River Conwy stands a picturesque old cottage with a pretty garden. Inside, all is low beams, old fireplaces and a traditional Welsh dresser. The menu is refreshingly local and the service is very welcoming.

What to see:
The River Conwy is at first wide and calm, later fast flowing and rock strewn. At Llanrwst, the bridge attributed to Inigo Jones, and the Tudor Gwydir castle are of interest. From here there are scenic drives to some of Snowdonia's most dramatic views. Driving east will bring you to the ancient cathedral of St Asaph and the Cefn Caves where once pre-historic men and animals lived.

The greatest wealth is contentment with a little.

INDEX

Abbey Tearooms Oxfordshire 111
Abbey Tea Room
                    Yorkshire (North) 150
Abbey Cottage   Scotland 158
Abbotsford House   Scotland 158
Acorn   Shropshire 114
Afonwen Craft &
  Antique Centre   Wales 166
Andrews Hotel   Oxfordshire 111
Annie's   Oxfordshire 112
Ann's Pantry   Gloucestershire 54
Antiques &
  Teas at Turnpike
  Cottage   Cornwall 21
Apothocoffee Shop
                Northamptonshire 104
April Cottage   Sussex (East) 138
Argyll Tea Room   Scotland 164
Ashwood   Yorkshire (West) 156
Aster's Tea Shop   Surrey 135
Audrey's   Wiltshire 147
Bailey's   Suffolk 130
Bank Cottage   Wales 167
Bartley Mill   Kent 71
Battlers Green   Hertfordshire 65
Batwing   Isle of Wight 68
Beam Ends   Sussex (West) 139
Belsay Hall   Northumberland 107
Betty's   Yorkshire (North) 150
Black Cat   Gloucestershire 55
Blackmore's Bookshop
  Tea Rooms   120
Black's Tea Rooms   Scotland 159
Blake House   Essex 50
Bolton Abbey Tea
  Cottage   Yorkshire (North) 151
Boscobel House   Shropshire 118
Brambles   Scotland 159
Brethren's Kitchen
                    Warwickshire 145
Bridge Tea Rooms   Wiltshire 146
Bridgecombe Farm
                    Oxfordshire 112
Brighstone Tea
  Gardens   Isle of Wight 69
Brownside Coach
  House   Cumbria 25
Buckfast Abbey   Devon 37
Bumble   Wales 167
Burgers   Buckinghamshire 13
Burgh House   London 85
Bush House   Hampshire 59
Butcher's Mere   Kent 71
Cake Table   Essex 51
Caledonian Hotel   Scotland 160
Cannizaro House   London 93
Caroline's Pantry   Cheshire 20
Carousel   Suffolk 130
Cassandra's Cup   Hampshire 59
Castle Tea Rooms
                    Hertfordshire 65
Castle Hotel   Somerset 120
Caudwell's Mill   Derbyshire 33
Causeway Tea Cottage Essex 50
Celtic Fare Tea Rooms   Wales 168

Chantry Tea Rooms
                  Northumberland 108
Chatsworth   Derbyshire 33
Chaunt House   Sussex (East) 140
Chelsea Physic Garden
                         London 90
Chenies Manor
                 Buckinghamshire 13
Cherry Trees Tea Gallery
                            Kent 73
Cherubs   Kent 73
Chesters   Cumbria 25
Chester Grosvenor   Cheshire 20
Church   Hertfordshire 66
Claridge's   London 94
Claris's   Kent 74
Claydon House
                 Buckinghamshire 14
Cloister Restaurant Somerset 121
Clun Bridge Tea
  Rooms   Shropshire 115
Cobbled Way   Yorkshire (West) 157
Cobweb   Hampshire 60
Coffee Shop   London 94
College Farm   London 83
Compleat Angler Hotel
                 Buckinghamshire 14
Copper Kettle   Kent 74
Copper Kettle Northumberland 109
Copperfield's   Bedfordshire 9
Copshaw Kitchen   Scotland 160
Corn Dolly   Devon 38
Cosy Corner   Wales 168
Cosy Teapot   Devon 38
Cottage Tea Room   Derbyshire 35
Cromwell Eating
  House   Yorkshire (North) 151
Crooked Cottage   Essex 51
Crypt, St Martin-in-the-Fields
                         London 99
Curtis's   Suffolk 131
De Grey's   Shropshire 115
Dent Crafts Centre   Cumbria 27
De Wynn's   Cornwall 22
Dove Cottage   Cumbria 27
Drover's Rest
  Tea Rooms   Wales 169
Drury House   Berkshire 10
Duncombe Park
                Yorkshire (North) 153
Edgcumbe Arms   Cornwall 22
Elan Arts Centre   Kent 75
Elms   Hereford & Worcester 63
Emporia Armani   London 90
Essex Rose   Essex 53
Exceat Farmhouse
                  Sussex (East) 138
Eyam Tea Room   Derbyshire 35
Fir Tree House   Kent 75
Forest Tea House   Hampshire 60
Fortnum & Mason   London 95
Four and Twenty
  Blackbirds   Devon 39
Gainsborough Old Hall
                   Lincolnshire 81

George of Stamford
  Hotel   Lincolnshire 81
Georgian Coffee
  House   Buckinghamshire 15
Georgian Tea Rooms   Devon 39
Georgian Tea Room   Dorset 46
Gilly's   Isle of Wight 69
Gingerbread Shop   Derbyshire 36
Gladstone Pottery
  Museum   Staffordshire 126
Gliffaes Hotel   Wales 169
Gomshall Mill   Surrey 135
Granary   Suffolk 131
Grandy Nook   Cumbria 28
Green Shutter   Scotland 161
Greys Dining Room   Devon 40
Greystones   Staffordshire 126
Hampstead
  Tea Rooms   London 85
Harrods   London 89
Holdenby House
                Northamptonshire 105
Hoo Farm   Shropshire 117
Honeybees   Devon 40
Hopechest   Derbyshire 36
Horse with the
  Red Umbrella   Dorset 47
Hyde Park Hotel   London 89
Jenny Traditional
  Tea Rooms   Scotland 161
Jenny Wren   Gloucestershire 55
Jessica's Tea
  Shop   Northamptonshire 105
Jireh House   Isle of Wight 70
Joyce's-on-the-Chart   Surrey 136
Kailzie Gardens   Scotland 163
Kerry House Tea Rooms
                    Warwickshire 145
Kettle   Devon 41
Kind Kyttock's   Scotland 163
King Alfred's Kitchen   Dorset 47
King John's
  Hunting Lodge   Wiltshire 147
Knollys   Sussex (East) 140
Lace Hall   Nottinghamshire 110
Lake Vyrnwy   Wales 170
Lanesborough Hotel   London 87
Liberty's   London 95
Lockside Tea Room   Cheshire 21
Longdale Rural
  Craft Centre Nottinghamshire 110
Louis Patisserie   London 86
Lowerbourne House   Somerset 121
Magpie Café   Yorkshire (North) 153
Maison Bertaux   London 97
Maison Sagne   London 97
Malthouse   Shropshire 117
Manor Farm   Hampshire 61

INDEX

Manor Farm Craft Centre
                    Surrey 136
Marigold Cottage   Dorset 48
Market Place Teashop
            Co Durham 24
Marsh Farm   Staffordshire 127
Marshmallow Gloucestershire 56
Mary's   Suffolk 133
Mearsdon Manor   Devon 41
Michael Snell   Wiltshire 148
Mill Hotel   Suffolk 133
Miller Howe Hotel   Cumbria 28
Miss Marple Tea Shoppe
           Oxfordshire 113
Mistress Quickly Warwickshire 146
Mock Turtle   Sussex (East) 141
Montacute House Somerset 122
Mortons House Hotel Dorset 48
Mrs Pickwick   Avon 7
Mulberries Yorkshire (North) 154
Mulberry Room   Devon 43
Museum of Garden
  History   London 86
Myrtle Tree Buckinghamshire 17
Natashas   London 93
Needles & Nosh Lincolnshire 82
Norfolk Lavender   Norfolk 101
Oaklands   Wales 170
Ogmore Farm   Wales 171
Old Bakehouse   Somerset 122
Old Barn   Norfolk 102
Old Bridge Hotel
        Cambridgeshire 18
Old Clockhouse   Devon 43
Old Jordans Buckinghamshire 15
Old Lady Tea Shop
        Gloucestershire 57
Old Post House Sussex (East) 141
Old Post Office
  Tea Rooms Staffordshire 129
Old School Tea Rooms
          Scotland 164
Old Swan   Hertfordshire 66
Old Thatch Tea Shop
       Isle of Wight 70
Old Warehouse   Suffolk 134
Olde Bakery Gloucestershire 56
Original Maids
  of Honour Tearoom Surrey 137
Owl Tea Rooms   Norfolk 102
Passiflora   Staffordshire 127
Past Times   Devon 44
Peggoty's Tea Shoppe Kent 76
Peg Woffington Cottage
           London 101
Perfect Setting Cambridgeshire 18
Periwinkle Cottage Somerset 123
Peter de Wit   London 87

Philpott's   Essex 53
Pinnacle Café   Wales 171
Plas   Wales 172
Plas-Glyn-y-Weddw
  Gallery   Wales 173
Polly Tea Rooms Wiltshire 148
Poppy's &
  The Stables Shropshire 118
Potter In   Dorset 49
Powis Castle   Wales 172
Primrose Cottage   Devon 44
Primrose Patisserie London 84
Pump Room   Avon 7
Queen Elizabeth's Guest
  Chamber   Kent 76
Rainbows   Bedfordshire 9
Randolph Hotel Oxfordshire 114
Restaurant at
  Thomas Goode London 98
Richoux   London 91
Ritz Hotel   London 98
Rococo Rooms, Williams &
  Williams   Shropshire 119
Rose Cottage Derbyshire 37
Rosie Lee's   Oxfordshire 113
Roses   Kent 77
Rothay Manor   Cumbria 29
Royal Clarence Hotel Devon 45
Rumballs   Hertfordshire 67
Sail Loft   Cornwall 23
Sally Lunn's House   Avon 8
Sandbach   Wales 173
Savoy Hotel   London 100
Sentry Box   Kent 77
Settle   Somerset 123
Sharon's Pantry   Norfolk 103
Sharrow Bay Hotel Cumbria 29
Sheila's Cottage   Cumbria 30
Shepherd's Sussex (West) 143
Shepherd's Hall
      Yorkshire (North) 154
Sissinghurst Granary Kent 78
Six Ashes Tea
  Rooms   Shropshire 119
Slepe Cottage   Dorset 49
Small Talk Gloucestershire 57
Soup Kitchen Staffordshire 128
Splashes Tea Shoppe
          Hampshire 61
Stables Queen's Court
          Scotland 165
St Martin's Tea
  Rooms Sussex (West) 143
Steeplegate Cambridgeshire 19
Still Too Few   London 99
Stokes   Lincolnshire 82
Ston Easton Park   Avon 8
Stones   Wiltshire 149
Stone Close   Cumbria 30
Stonehouse Bakery
      Yorkshire (North) 155
Stravinsky's
  Russian Tea House London 92

Strawberry Tree Bedfordshire 10
Sugar 'n' Spice
     Hereford & Worcester 64
Swanbourne Cottage
      Buckinghamshire 17
Swan Cottage Sussex (East) 144
Swinsty Tea Garden
     Yorkshire (North) 155
Taylor's Tea Rooms
     Yorkshire (North) 156
Tea at Peg's Gloucestershire 58
Tea Cosy   Berkshire 11
Tea Cosy Tea Rooms
      Northumberland 108
Tea Gallery   London 92
Tea House   Kent 78
Teapots Northamptonshire 107
Tea Room Cambridgeshire 19
Tea Shoppe   Somerset 125
Tea Time   London 91
Tealby Tea Rooms
       Lincolnshire 83
Teazzells Tea Rooms
      Staffordshire 128
Thatched Cottage Devon 45
Tickle Manor   Suffolk 134
Tiffins   Kent 79
Tintern Station   Wales 174
Tisanes Hereford & Worcester 64
Traquair House Scotland 165
Tregain Tea Room Cornwall 23
Trelissick Gardens Cornwall 24
Tudor House Sussex (East) 139
Tu Hwnt I'r Bont Wales 174
Tutti Pole   Berkshire 11
Two Tees   Essex 54
Village Bakery   Cumbria 31
Village Tea Rooms Hampshire 63
Village Tea Shop   Kent 79
Waldorf Hotel   London 100
Water Mill Hertfordshire 67
Watts Gallery   Surrey 137
Whalebone House Norfolk 103
Whiddons   Devon 46
White Monk Northumberland 109
Whitmore Gallery Staffordshire 129
Wild Strawberry Cumbria 31
Willow Tea Room Scotland 166
Willow Tea
  Room   Sussex (East) 144
Wiltshire Kitchen Wiltshire 149
Windmill Tea Room Norfolk 104
Wintor House Gloucestershire 58
Wishing Well Hertfordshire 68
Wishing Well Tea
  Rooms   Somerset 125
Wisteria Tea Rooms London 84
Wrinkled Stocking
      Yorkshire (West) 157
Wythop Mill   Cumbria 32
Ye Olde Copper Kettle
         Cumbria 32